THE DRAWINGS

OF

HANS HOLBEIN

IN THE COLLECTION OF

HIS MAJESTY THE KING

AT WINDSOR CASTLE

by

K. T. PARKER

OXFORD & LONDON

THE PHAIDON PRESS LTD

1945

The reproductions in this Volume are from a new
set of photographs taken by Mr. Alfred Carlebach

1945
MADE IN GREAT BRITAIN
PRINTED AT THE BAYNARD PRESS · LONDON

SOLOMON AND THE QUEEN OF SHEBA

THE DRAWINGS OF
HANS HOLBEIN
AT WINDSOR CASTLE

PHAIDON PRESS
1945

FOREWORD

WHEN THE WINDSOR HOLBEINS are next studied in detail, it is to be hoped that it will be possible to examine them under infra-red and ultra-violet rays. Whether anything of interest would show itself, whether what might show itself would be usefully interpretable, is far too uncertain to forecast. But the test should be made, and no doubt in time it will be made and duly recorded. At the present juncture facilities are not available, and so the matter had to be shelved. Nor was it possible to see the backs of the drawings, and to go into the question of their watermarks. For information on this topic, the reader must be referred to Professor Paul Ganz's *Kritischer Katalog*, where relevant matter is to be found. But since the author of the present catalogue could contribute nothing of his own on this point, and since such data as he might have taken over could not be checked, it was thought better to leave the matter aside altogether. Wartime is unfavourable to research, and problems which normally it would be a plain duty to investigate, must needs be postponed to a more propitious future. The present publication, for which, incidentally, the initiative came not from the author, but from the publishers acting in agreement with His Majesty's Librarian, though it changed its aims and viewpoint not a little in the course of preparation, remained, as it started, a wartime undertaking.

The scope of the book is a trifle wider than its title would imply. It embraces the whole of the present Holbein series without exception; and two further drawings, though not reproduced, have at least been discussed, in spite of the fact that they were rightly eliminated from the series during the last century as having no relevance, other than traditional, with Holbein. The arrangement of the plates is in the main chronological, but another factor had constantly to be borne in mind: the fact that the plates appear grouped in pairs, face-to-face. So far as possible, the scale of reduction was kept consistent and proportional. A convenient way of judging the relative sizes of any two drawings is to compare the mark of the Royal Collection which is impressed in each case in the right lower corner.

Among those who in various ways have been helpful to the author in the course of his work, Sir Owen Morshead, in whose charge the drawings are, must, of course, be mentioned first. He not only gave assistance however and whenever it was asked for, but contributed many useful notes and suggestions of his own accord. Mr. Martin Davies, too, has shown great kindness and patience. Others to whom thanks and gratitude are due and whose names should not be omitted, include Dr. Otto Pächt, Mr. Denys Sutton, Mr. S. Gibson, Mr. A. J. Collins, Father B. C. Gurrin, S.J., Professor Randolph Schwabe, Mr. T. Lowinsky and Mr. L. Goldscheider.

K. T. P.

SIR JOHN GODSALVE (DETAIL OF NO. 22, ORIGINAL SIZE)

INTRODUCTION

IN a volume such as this, dealing on specialized lines with Holbein's drawings in the Royal Collection, it will be well to start by giving some account of their long and adventurous wanderings, a veritable Odyssey through the centuries. Not that the relevant information were lacking elsewhere, or had hitherto only been given in a disconnected form. To justify going over the ground again, if justification indeed were needed, it would be enough to point to the many minor inaccuracies, and occasional major ones, which occur in every printed account of the drawings. Let us start therefore by dealing, as fully as space will permit, with their history, and first of all pause, for a moment at least, at the point soon after the accession of George II, when Queen Caroline discovered them, a long-forgotten treasure, in a bureau in Kensington Palace. That incident, as no other, marks a dividing line between two distinct phases of their existence. From that moment onwards the full light of modern times rests upon them, and they emerge once and for all from the absorbing, but often confused chapter of their history, during which, more than once, all recorded traces of their whereabouts fade out, and they are lost from sight for decades at a stretch.

The part played by Queen Caroline in the discovery is by no means merely legendary. It is abundantly vouched for by Vertue[1] and others, and there is every reason to believe that it was in fact by her, at Kensington, and in 1727, that the Windsor Holbeins (then a collection bound together in form of a book) were brought to light. This familiar anecdote, nevertheless, has been romanticized and misrepresented, and needs to be seen afresh in its true perspective. The fact is that Queen Caroline found far more than she knew, in other words that she discovered far less than she found. For the contents of the bureau was not merely the one priceless treasure which concerns us here, but included the no less celebrated book of drawings by Leonardo, and many more besides by various masters. What Queen Caroline found was not a single item, mislaid or forgotten, but a collection, dating back to Stuart times, of considerable size and diversity. Among the miscellaneous MSS. in the British Museum is an inventory of the reign of George II[2] listing these 'Books of drawings and Prints in the Buroe in His Majesty's Great Closset at Kensington,' and though it could be argued that not all the items mentioned in it were necessarily there in 1727, it is yet more than probable that such was the case. Vertue's anecdote thus assumes an altogether new complexion, and as the measure of Queen Caroline's good fortune waxes, that of her sagacity and discernment wanes. Her complete apathy to all but the work of her great compatriot is, indeed, no less extraordinary in its way than the appreciation which she bestowed so enthusiastically upon him. So it came about that for many years more the Leonardos lay forgotten and neglected; not till early in the following reign, about 1760, were they well and truly discovered by Richard Dalton, Librarian to George III[3]. Queen Caroline, no doubt, had seen the volume, but the statement of such writers as Richard Holmes[4] and A. B. Chamberlain[5] that it was discovered by her along with the other is too misleading to be countenanced. To Dalton belongs the credit for the one discovery as certainly as it does to Queen Caroline for the other. The credit of a double discovery is the due of neither. But this has been claimed not only in the Queen's favour, it has also been hinted at in Dalton's, with the only difference that in this latter case the error is too obvious to be misleading. Here one may readily detect a distortion of the none too accurate account given by Charles Rogers of the finding of the Leonardos in a 'large and strong chest,'[6] in which, he says, the Holbeins had also

---

[1]See *Walpole Society Publ.*, Vol. xx (1931/32), p. 3; Walpole, *Anecdotes of Painting in England*, ed. Dallaway-Wornum, 1862, p.84. [2]*Burlington Magazine*, Vol. LXVI (1935), p.223. [3]*Fine Arts Quarterly Review*, Vol. I (1863), p.263. [4]*Portraits of Illustrious Personages of the Court of Henry VIII* (Hanfstaengl), s.a., Vol. I, p.3. [5]*Hans Holbein the Younger*, 1913, Vol. II, p 249. [6]*A Collection of Prints in Imitation of Drawings*, 1778, p.4.

been concealed. In Dalton's day, of course, the latter had long since been removed,—but not from the supposititious chest, nor from a 'common table drawer' as is elsewhere stated, but from the Kensington bureau which, all too superficially, Queen Caroline had explored.

How did this great collection of Holbein's drawings come together in the first place? To what process of accretion does it owe its numbers and uniform character? To answer this, it is to the life-time of the artist himself that we must turn back, just as in the case of that other, even more comprehensive collection at Basel. But the genesis of the two collections differs, nevertheless, essentially. For whereas at Basel it was due to an insatiable urge for collecting on the part of a contemporary admirer that, by degrees, a matchless series of Holbein's work came into being[1], the Windsor contingent, or at least the bulk of it, was a natural and self-formed unit, being simply a part of that gradual accumulation of working material which piles up in every artist's studio, though it seldom remains so undisturbed and undispersed. There will be occasion later to stress the purely practical use which all these portrait studies were designed to serve. What matters at this stage is that the eighty odd drawings at Windsor, or the great majority of them, were not brought together piecemeal and selectively. Everything points to their having remained to the end in the artist's possession, and to have been together in his studio when, unaware of his approaching end, he turned the key in the door for the last time. Holbein's death, it will be recalled, was due to the plague, and overtook him abruptly, at the height of his reputation and activity. His last dispositions show signs of hurried transaction, and the Whitehall painting room, with all its contents and effects, was doubtless left by him just as it stood after any normal day of work.

For nearly a decade after 1543, the year in which Holbein died, there is nothing to tell us what became of the drawings. Nor is it easy even to bridge this interval with reasonable conjecture or surmise. On the assumption, however, a fairly safe one, that at the artist's death they were in Whitehall, on royal premises, the possibility should not be overlooked that they were absorbed forthwith into Crown property. This is possible, but hardly probable. For, to begin with, no mention of them occurs in the 1547 inventory of Crown effects[2], a likely source of information had they in fact been so appropriated, and not dealt with by the artist's executors charged with the duty of settling his estate and outstanding debts. Furthermore, by combining the evidence of two existing records, it appears probable that they were actually purchased for the Crown under Edward VI. Between 1543 and a date roughly about 1550, the whereabouts of the drawings must be accounted a mystery, but there seems no sufficient justification for including in the list of their one-time owners the sovereign whose Court they so vividly portray.

If an element of uncertainty remains, not as to Edward's ownership, but as to the purchase of the drawings during Edward's reign, the reason rightly admissible for such doubt involves a different argument from that which has up to now been supported. Of the two records to be considered, the first consists of an undated entry of expenditure in the accounts of Sir Thomas Carwarden, Master of the Revels to Edward VI, and reads: 'Item, for a peynted booke of Mr. Hanse Holby making 6 li.'[3] Against the obvious interpretation of this note that the payment in question covered the purchase of the book, it has been objected that the outlay was merely for the binding of it[4], in which case, of course, the possibility would remain that its contents had come to Edward not by purchase, but by succession. This reading, however, not only conflicts with the straightforward statement of the entry itself, but is irreconcilable with the sum of money involved, even supposing

---

[1]Paul Ganz, *Handzeichnungen H. Holbeins d.J.: Kritischer Katalog*, 1937, p.xii. [2]See W. A. Shaw, *Three Inventories of Pictures in the Collections of Henry VIII and Edward VI*, 1937. [3]Quoted from Losely MSS. by A. B. Chamberlain, *op. cit.*, Vol. ii, p.244. [4]Paul Ganz, *Kritischer Katalog*, 1937, p.xiv.

A WOMAN : UNKNOWN (DETAIL OF NO. 9, ORIGINAL SIZE)

the binding to have been of unusually sumptuous workmanship[1]. A question far more to the point
is whether really this 'peynted book' consisted, in part or whole, of the Windsor drawings. It would
clearly be rash to conclude that the 'peynted book' was identical with the 'great Booke,' of which
henceforth we shall hear so much, but for the fact that the second of the two records bearing
upon the question under consideration testifies beyond all doubt that the drawings were Crown
property in Edward's reign.

The special importance of this further document[2] does not end with the corroboration it provides
to Carwarden's entry. It gives not merely the proof of royal ownership of the drawings in Tudor times,
but carries forward the narrative of their history a further stage altogether to the first of two periods,
both of considerable duration, when they became alienated from the Crown, only to be retrieved
at a later date by a chain of fortunate circumstances. The document in question is the property of
Lord Scarborough, and consists of an inventory 'of the goods of John, Lord Lumly,' compiled in
1590, and mentioning 'a great Booke of Pictures doone by Haunce Holbyn of certyne Lordes,
Ladyes, gentlemen and gentlewomen of King Henry the 8 his tyme . . . which booke was King
Edward the 6.' At the time of the compilation of this inventory Lord Lumley had enjoyed possession
of the book for exactly ten years, for he had inherited it at the death of his father-in-law, Henry
FitzAlan, Earl of Arundel, in 1580[3]. How FitzAlan had become possessed of it from Edward VI, at
whose Court he had officiated as Lord Chamberlain, is not so clear ; but it seems that at the King's
death in 1553, the book, along with other artistic property, passed to him either by gift or purchase,
and found a home for the time being at Nonesuch. Whether it remained there after the palace was
ceded to Queen Elizabeth in 1590, or whether it was then removed to Lumley House on Tower
Hill, or to Lumley Castle, Co. Durham, does not emerge. So much is certain: that the information
concerning the drawings in the Lumley inventory is of a thoroughly reliable kind, coming, as it
does, from Henry FitzAlan, whose interest in Holbein, like that of the later Earl of Arundel, was
profound. The reference in the inventory will come under further notice[4] when the question of the
inscriptions on the drawings is discussed. So far it has been quoted only in its bearing on the present
theme of ownership.

At Lumley's death in 1609 the drawings once again found their way into royal possession, and
later, though not for long, into possession of the Crown. But before attempting to trace, as well as
may be, the actual course they took, we should first dispose of a fiction, constantly repeated though
devoid of all foundation, for the origin of which Vertue and Walpole must be held responsible.[5] It
affirms that 'after Holbein's death' the book was 'sold into France,' and there remained until the
time of Charles I, when it was brought back to this country by a Frenchman named de Liancourt[6],
who, it is alleged, ceded it to the King. It is easy to trace the source of this error to Vanderdoort's
catalogue of 1636 of King Charles' Collection[7], or rather to an absurd confusion between two per-
fectly blameless entries in that catalogue. Thus, as No. 42 of his inventory, Vanderdoort lists a book
of forty-nine portraits 'in dry colours of the chiefest Nobility and famous Men at that time in France',
stating that it was bought by the King from the 'Frenchman who brought the St. John of Leonard de
Vincia,' he, as noted elsewhere, being the aforesaid de Liancourt. It is obvious from the very outset
that the description of the book as a collection of French portraits invalidates the identification with

[1]See Cyril Davenport, *Thomas Berthelet*, 1901, p.35, quoting a bill (British Museum, Add. MS. 28, 196), giving
particulars of the cost of royal bindings supplied between 1541/43. [2]See *Walpole Society Publ.*, Vol. vi (1917/18), p.27.
[3]See M. F. S. Hervey, *Life of Thomas Howard, Earl of Arundel*, 1921, pp.52 seq. [4]See below, p. 22. [5]*Anecdotes of Painting*,
ed. Dallaway-Wornum, 1862, Vol. i, p.85, note 1. [6]He is frequently described in error as the 'Ambassador' of France.
There was no ambassador of that name at the time in question ; see C. H. Firth and S. C. Lomas, *Notes on the Diplomatic
Relations of England and France, 1603-1668*, 1906. [7]*A Catalogue and Description of King Charles the First's Capital Collection,
etc.*, London, 1757. Vanderdoort's preliminary draft and final MS. are both in the Bodleian Library.

WILLIAM WARHAM, ARCHBISHOP OF CANTERBURY (DETAIL OF NO. 12, ORIGINAL SIZE)

Holbein's Great Booke. But not only that: the Holbein book, under item 14, is itself specifically alluded to by Vanderdoort as having been ceded by the King to a fellow collector in return for a picture by Raphael, to which the catalogue entry refers. The passage, a keystone in our narrative, is as follows: 'Item A little St. George which the King had in exchange of my Lord Chamberlain, Earl of Pembroke, for the book of Holbein's drawings; wherein are many heads, which were done with Crayons, which my Lord Chamberlain immediately so soon as he received it of the King, gave it to my Lord Marshal. . . .' At its very source, therefore, the contention that the drawings were for a time in French possession shows itself to be worthless, and indirectly we gain the further piece of important information, that, after belonging to King Charles, the book again passed out of Crown ownership, changing hands rapidly between Lord Pembroke and the great Earl of Arundel.

Turning back to the time of Lumley's death, one must admit, however, that the next link in the chain of ownership after 1609 is not as clear as one would wish. In spite of the circumstantial nature of Vanderdoort's account of Lord Pembroke's exchange, so distinguished a scholar as Lionel Cust[1] has suggested that the drawings were among a number of Lumley art treasures which passed direct to Thomas Howard, Earl of Arundel, the great collector and connoisseur, who, in default of surviving Lumley issue and as a great-grandson on the distaff side of Henry FitzAlan, was in line of succession to Lord Lumley's inheritance from his father-in-law. But for more reasons than one this theory must be rejected. To begin with, Vanderdoort's evidence cannot lightly be brushed aside ; it is significant, moreover, that no allusion to portrait drawings by Holbein is to be found in Joachim von Sandrart's detailed and informative account of a visit to the Arundel Collection in 1627[2]. Nor should the interesting fact be overlooked that a portrait study by Holbein of Lord Abergavenny[3] is to this day at Wilton in Pembroke possession. Is it not extremely probable that the drawing was detached from the book during its brief passage (reported by Vanderdoort, but disallowed by Cust) through the then Lord Pembroke's collection ?

Though tangible proof is not available, it is far more plausible that the Great Booke, whose wanderings we are endeavouring to trace, was included in a part of the Lumley library which, after 1609, was acquired by Prince Henry of Wales, elder son of James I[4]. At the premature death of that gifted prince in 1612, the library, and with it, presumably, the Great Booke, seems to have passed to his brother, afterwards King Charles, and with him the drawings remained for some fifteen years before next changing ownership as the result of the transaction with Lord Pembroke. The *St. George* by Raphael, for which the King ceded the Holbeins, is, as everyone knows, the picture commissioned by Guidobaldo da Montefeltro for presentation to Henry VII after the former had been invested with the Order of the Garter. After the Commonwealth it passed through various French collections, later to the Hermitage, and in recent years to Mr. Andrew Mellon and the National Gallery at Washington, D.C. An engraving of it by Lucas Vorstermann the Younger[5], shows it to have been in Lord Pembroke's hands as late as 1627. The exchange must therefore have been made at a date not precisely ascertainable between 1627 and 1630, the latter being the year of Pembroke's death[6].

So far, then, our survey has covered some eighty years, during which seven successive owners

[1] *Walpole Society Publ.*, Vol. vi (1917/18), p. 18. [2] *Teutsche Akademie*, 1675, Vol. i, p.251. [3] *Ganz* 37 (xxxvi, 4). [4] See *Burlington Magazine*, Vol. xviii (1911), p.219, and M. F. S. Hervey, *op. cit.*, p.60. [5] Repr. by Claude Phillips, *The Picture Gallery of Charles I*, 1896, p.79. [6] Since the above was written, Mr. L. Goldscheider has pointed out that in the Catalogue of the Hermitage Gallery (ed. 1891, p.139) the date of the exchange is stated to be as late as 1639. On reconsidering all the evidence it does become evident that it is impossible to uphold the year 1630 as a definite *terminus ante quem*. For in 1626 Philip, afterwards fourth Earl of Pembroke, succeeded his brother William, the third Earl, as Lord Chamberlain of the Household. Vanderdoort's reference to ' my Lord Chamberlain ' can therefore refer to either. The really vital date to establish would be that of the earlier version of Norgate's *Discourse;* see below, p. 16. But as the approximate year of the Pembroke exchange, 1630 holds good.

THOMAS, LORD VAUX (DETAIL OF NO. 24, ORIGINAL SIZE)

have been identified. Of these, only FitzAlan and Lumley enjoyed their treasure for any great length of time, in each case a period of roughly a quarter of a century. King Charles' term was shorter by about ten years, while both Edward VI and Prince Henry of Wales had but brief tenures of ownership. The briefest of all, however, was evidently Pembroke's, for as we know he forthwith passed on the book to Thomas Howard, his brother-in-law. Of the circumstances of this princely gift nothing in detail is known, but it is obvious that the drawings must long have been the object of interest and admiration to so ardent an admirer of Holbein, a collector whose great-uncle and great-grandfather before him had owned the book, and whose forbears appear among the personages portrayed. But let no one be deluded into believing the fiction (for such it is) of Arundel's persistent attempts to buy the drawings while they were still the King's, nor of Charles' extortionate demands, having agreed at last to part with them[1]. Surely there was nothing of avarice in Charles' nature; and of Arundel it was said by a contemporary that he 'knew and kept greater distance toward his Sovereign than any person'[2]. The story does not ring true from the start, and on scrutiny it turns out to be simply the misread substance of a letter, rather involved in its phrasing, addressed by Arundel on 25 April, 1629, to Sir Henry Vane, 'His Majesty's Cofferer', then at The Hague[3]. What it refers to in reality are negotiations conducted by Vane simultaneously on behalf of the King and of Lord Arundel, the former wishing to buy from a certain Dutchman a picture, and the latter a book of drawings by Holbein[4]. This coveted book, whatever it was, had certainly nothing to do with the Great Booke, and being so, it would be idle to pursue the matter to greater length.

There is evidence of two kinds, pictorial and literary, of the passage of the drawings through the Arundel Collection. Of the former class are a number of etchings by Wenceslas Hollar, but though these include a number of familiar faces, and are duly inscribed *ex collectione Arundeliana*, their interest to us is comparatively small. Since no precise indication of the technique of the originals is given, the possibility cannot be set aside that their immediate antecedents were pictures or miniatures based upon the drawings, and not the actual drawings themselves. This is indeed probably true in some cases; on the other hand it is not easy to believe that, for instance, the print corresponding with No. 8 of our series[5] was otherwise than based directly upon it. It would be a strange coincidence, too, if in the case of a number of etchings having the appearance of medallion miniatures[6], the exemplar in miniature form had in each case disappeared, while the drawing itself had in each case survived. It seems likely that Hollar, though faithful in portraiture, did thus occasionally modify the appearance of the originals from which he worked. More reliable than these pictorial sources are the literary, and here we have in particular the discourse of Edward Norgate, entitled *Miniatura or the Art of Limning*[7], that merits our careful attention and study. Norgate, himself much indebted to Nicholas Hilliard, was followed in close dependence by certain minor writers, and interesting information may be gleaned from their works as well, both on the history of the Great Booke and its contents.

An important part of Norgate's evidence is concerned with Holbein's technique and the much vexed question of the state of preservation of the drawings. More of this will be said in due course. The quotations about to be given will be clipped, so far as possible, to touch only upon the question of ownership. What gives Norgate his particular interest in this context is that not only have we

---

[1]Paul Ganz, *Kritischer Katalog*, 1937, p.xiv. [2]Edward Walker, *Life of Thomas Howard*, 1705, p.222. [3]Quoted in full by M. F. S. Hervey, *op. cit.*, p.286. [4]Or were both the projected purchases for the King? The point is somewhat ambiguous. M. F. S. Hervey (p.542) assumes the latter. [5]Parthey 1552 ; repr. *Klassiker der Kunst: Holbein*, p.196. [6]Parthey 1342, 1465, 1547, 1549; repr. *Klassiker der Kunst*, p.199. [7]Edited by Martin Hardie, and published in 1919 by the Clarendon Press.

WILLIAM RESKIMER (DETAIL OF NO. 31, ORIGINAL SIZE)

his original discourse in variant texts, but also pirated and derivative versions of it, which, though consisting largely of paraphrase and verbatim quotation, also contain independent information of a useful kind. Bearing in mind the various dates of composition or publication; the dates of the Earl and Countess of Arundel's deaths in 1646 and 1654 respectively; of the Restoration in 1660, and the death of Charles II in 1685, let the reader analyse for himself the following parallel extracts:

(1) Edward Norgate: *An exact & Compendious discours concerning the Art of Miniatura or Limning.* (Early Version, composed not before 1627 and probably not much later than 1630.) MS. Harleian 6000 in the British Museum.

'. . . . I shall not need to insist upon the particulars of this manner of working; it shall suffice if you please to view of a book of pictures by the life, by the incomparable Hans Holbein. . . . They are the pictures of most of the English Lords and Ladies then living. . . . The book hath been long a wanderer, but is now happily fallen into the hands of my noble lord the Earl Marshal' (i.e., the Earl of Arundel).

(2) Edward Norgate : *A Treatise on Miniature or the Arte of Limning* (Final version, composed about 1648/50). MS. Tanner 326 in the Bodleian Library.

'. . . Of this Kind was an excellent booke while it remained in the hands of the most noble Earl of Arundel and Surrey. But I heare it has been a great traveller, and wherever now, he hath got his errata. . .'

(3) Daniel King : *Miniatura or the Art of Limning.* (Pirated version of the earlier text of Norgate, after 1646.) Add. MS. 12461 in the British Museum.

'. . . The booke hath been a long time a wanderer, but is now happily fallen into the hands of the Noble Lord, the Earle Marshall, a most eminent patron to all painters who understood the art ; and who therefore preserved this book with his life, till both were lost together.'

(4) William Sanderson : *Graphice*, London, 1658.

'. . . After a long time of Peregrination, this book fell into the hands of the late Earle of Arundell, Earle Marshall of England, an eminent Patron to all Painters, and understood the Art; and therefore preserved this Book with his Life till both were lost together.'

(5) Alexander Browne : *Appendix to the Art of Painting in Miniature or Limning.* London, 1675.

'. . . The Book has long been a Wanderer, but is now happily fallen into the King's Collection.'

What is to be gathered from the above references, apart from the certainty that for a time the drawings were Arundel's? 'That the book was described [in (2)] as a *great traveller*,' writes A. B. Chamberlain,[1] is no doubt due to the fact that from 1642 until his death, four years later, the Earl was living on the Continent, and that he took all his works of art with him.' Specious as this interpretation is, it becomes clear from the corresponding phrase ('a wanderer') in the earlier text, composed long before Arundel's departure from England, that originally the author had in mind the book's vicissitudes and peregrinations before entering the Arundel Collection. It is true enough that among the art treasures that accompanied, or rather followed, the Earl and Countess into their voluntary exile, the Great Booke may very well have been included. But at best this

[1] *Op. cit.,* Vol. II, pp.247/8.

journey to Holland can only have added further colour to the 'wanderer' idea, and have influenced its retention in the final version of the discourse. In (3) and (4) the original meaning is once again clear, both texts alluding, as does (2), to Arundel's death, in the former case, incidentally, with a careless lack of co-ordination with the words immediately preceding. Norgate's later text, as well as King's and Sanderson's, make no disguise of their writers' ignorance as to the then whereabouts of the book. In (5), on the other hand, the same precision as in (1) recurs, but with a different message: here we learn that the drawings had once again returned to the Crown, though through what channels is unfortunately left unstated.

A theory conflicting with this statement of Alexander Browne was first put forward by the Rev. James Dallaway in his 1826 edition of Walpole's *Anecdotes*.[1] It claimed for James II, not his predecessor, the credit for the book's redemption, stating that the purchase was made in 1686 at a sale of the effects of Henry, Duke of Norfolk, and giving as evidence an unspecified note in the *London Gazette* of that year. As long ago as 1863, however, it was pointed out by B. B. Woodward[2] that neither in the *Gazette* of 1686 nor of the adjacent years could this vital entry be traced. Further search has now again proved fruitless, and it seems that Dallaway was not only unacquainted with the passage from Alexander Browne, but misinformed in regard to the notice alleged to be in the *Gazette*. It should not be overlooked, however, that confirmation for Browne's statement is not at present forthcoming: it stands on its merits as a contemporary record, with nothing in the least improbable about it, but lacking nevertheless the corroboration one would wish for, and might very reasonably expect to find.

Although dates occur on the relevant etchings of Hollar subsequent to the Earl's departure from England, proof has still to be produced that the Great Booke was in fact moved to the Continent. For could not these prints, assuming that they were actually based on the drawings themselves, have been engraved from preparatory copies made in England at an earlier date? The truth is that between about 1642 and 1727 there is practically nothing to add to the bare statement of the return of the drawings into Crown property which has been quoted above. It is known that in 1640 the Earl of Arundel drew up a will by which at his decease the collections were to pass to the Countess. Six years later, at Padua, Lord Arundel died, the Countess surviving him and continuing to reside in Holland. She settled, along with the collections, first at Amersfoort and later at Amsterdam. There, in 1654, she died intestate. Her only surviving son, Viscount Stafford, who was with her at Amsterdam, thereupon proceeded to pronounce a nuncupative will in his own favour, and to dispose of certain sections of the collection. Litigation followed at the instance of his nephews, Henry and Charles Howard. An inventory was drawn up in 1654 in this connexion[3], but it was incomplete and omitted the contents of a number of cases of which Lord Stafford had retained custody. The Great Booke is nowhere mentioned. Was it meanwhile in Lord Stafford's care? Had it already changed hands once again, perhaps even before the death of the Countess? Or can it have passed, at the Earl's death, not to the Countess at all, but as part of the Arundel library, to Henry Frederick, the next successor to the titles? To all these questions no satisfactory answer can at present be given. There is no phase in the history of the drawings so full of problems as that of the years immediately following upon Arundel's death.

Even the unconfirmed report, therefore, stating that by 1675 the drawings had returned into the Crown collection, is of particular value to us. A writer already quoted, B. B. Woodward, has suggested that the purchase may have been effected on Charles' II behalf by Sir Peter Lely, himself so distinguished a collector of drawings[4]. 'And it would be in perfect keeping,' he adds, 'with the

---

[1]Vol. I, p. 145. [2]*Fine Arts Quarterly Review*, Vol. I (1863), p. 264, note §. [3]*Burlington Magazine*, Vol. XIX (1911), pp.282/6. [4]*Fine Arts Quarterly Review*, Vol. I (1863), p.263.

King's well-known character that when acquired they should be put away in so careless a manner as to be, in effect, lost to the world for about half a century.' If the conjecture concerning Lely lacks tangible support, there is at least nothing inherently improbable about it. But for the rest, Woodward's reflections are demonstrably at fault, and for this once the Merry Monarch may be absolved of a charge of inconstancy. The truth is that, even though the book is not heard of again till Queen Caroline's time[1], it was meanwhile in its appropriate place, that is in the bureau serving as a receptacle for the royal collection of drawings[2]. To it, in due course, the Leonardos were added. The fact that the latter were not acquired before the reign of William III[3] is significant in this connexion, for it shows that even at so late a date as that, the earlier acquisitions were not yet in any sense lost or forgotten. From an interesting note in the diary of Viscount Percival, afterwards first Earl of Egmont[4], which seems to be based on information given to him personally by Queen Caroline in 1735, the Holbeins, before their removal to Kensington, had been at Whitehall, the very place where many of them were doubtless made. In Wolsey's ancient palace, it would appear, they survived the disastrous conflagration of 1698, in which Holbein's great painting in the Privy Chamber perished.

A further point of interest in Lord Egmont's note is that he expressly states that at the time of their discovery the drawings 'were in a book.' The Great Booke, therefore, was apparently still intact, a detail as to which Walpole's more ambiguous phrase, 'a curious parcel'[5], would have left us in doubt. Thus, for a further reason, not mentioned at the outset of this survey, the rediscovery of the drawings in 1727 was a dividing line in their history. For it was then that the grand old volume, after all its vicissitudes and with the memories of nearly two centuries attaching to it, was broken up—perhaps not to the detriment of the drawings it contained, but, let us frankly admit it, regrettably none the less. From that point onwards it is no longer the Great Booke that concerns us, but the drawings themselves, and their further history lies open before us. They were in 1728 glazed, framed, and delivered 'for her Maj^tys use' to Richmond Lodge, Queen Caroline's favourite residence, and there for a period of time they decorated the royal apartment. At Richmond Lord Egmont saw them in 1735; two years later Queen Caroline died. At a date not precisely recorded, but certainly after 1737, they were returned to Kensington and hung in what had been the Queen's closet,—'a very improper place' for their display, so Walpole assures us, 'some hanging against the light, or with scarce any, and some so high as not to be discernible'[6]. A catalogue compiled by Vertue in 1743 was published in 1758, including engraved diagrams showing the position of each drawing on the wall[7]. While it lasted, the Kensington Holbein Room was something of a memorial both to Caroline of Ansbach and the artist himself. But in the following reign a new course was

[1]Since the above was written, an interesting passage from the Diary of Constantine Huygens has been published in the *Burlington Magazine* (Vol. LXXXV, 1944, p.225). This records how Huygens, on 1 September, 1690, was summoned by Queen Mary to inspect the volumes both of Leonardo's and Holbein's drawings. [2]A writing cabinet with boulle and marquetry inlay, formerly in the Queen's Closet, Kensington, now in the Eighteenth-Century Room, Buckingham Palace, has been conjectured to be the historic bureau; see H. Clifford Smith, *Buckingham Palace*, 1931, p.78, note 2, and plate 254. But surely this cannot be correct. It could not possibly have held the books listed in the inventory (above, p. 7); nor, indeed, was it ever said that the bureau was in the Queen's Closet. The Holbeins hung there, on the walls; but the bureau stood in the King's Great Closet, afterwards being relegated to the Wardrobe. [3]K. Clark, *Catalogue of the Collection of Drawings of Leonardo da Vinci at Windsor Castle*, 1935, p.XII. [4]*Historical MSS. Commission: Report on the MSS. of the Earl of Egmont*, Vol. II (1923), p.190. [5]*Catalogue of the Collection of Pictures, etc., belonging to King James II*, 1758, p.iii. [6]*Anecdotes of Painting*, ed. Dallaway-Wornum, 1862, Vol. I, p.85, note 5. [7]*A Catalogue of the Collection of Pictures, etc., belonging to King James II, to which is added a Catalogue of the Pictures and Drawings in the Closet of the Late Queen Caroline*. Vertue's catalogue lists 90 items (not 89, as stated by Walpole), of which Nos. 100, 102 and 197 have yet to be satisfactorily accounted for, though P. Ganz (*Kritischer Katalog*, 1937, p.XV) asserts that all are still traceable in the present collection. The engraved diagram shows (though this is not mentioned in the text of the catalogue) that No. 102 was dated 1531. One may reasonably infer that the attribution to Holbein was incorrect, since dates do not occur on his authentic drawings. A work of 1531, moreover, would ill accord with the uniformly English character of the series. Of No. 197 (unnamed; $14\frac{3}{4} \times 10\frac{3}{4}$ in.) it may be significant that the marginal note in the catalogue describes it

QUEEN JANE SEYMOUR (DETAIL OF NO. 39, ORIGINAL SIZE)

adopted: the drawings were 'released' from their frames, and returned once again into book form. On this occasion two volumes were decided upon; their then haphazard order, a classification by sexes, is recorded by Wornum[8] from a MS. list, said to be in the Royal Library. Another such list among the papers at Windsor, shows that at a somewhat later date a more intelligent arrangement, again in two volumes, was made. In the 1760's, when much of the contents of other royal residences was assembled to furnish Buckingham House[9], the drawings were for the second time removed from Kensington, where now they had remained for roughly a quarter of a century. Under Queen Victoria they moved again, this time from London to Windsor. A safer method of mounting having meanwhile been adopted, the many changes of place, of treatment and of owner- ship that they had experienced, seemed at long last to be over. But yet another move was necessitated by the events of yesterday, and at the moment of writing a secluded spot among the mountains of Wales is the war-time refuge of this great national treasure.

*   *   *   *

The publication between 1792 and 1800 of the well-known series of stipple engravings by Francesco Bartolozzi was another landmark in the history of the drawings. It was Queen Caroline's discovery that first revealed the treasure; long after, in 1890, the Tudor Exhibition at the New Gallery was first to bring the originals to the sight of a select public. But it was the prints, executed under the direction of John Chamberlaine[10], Dalton's successor as Librarian to George III, which truly popularized them and introduced their presence into the houses and homes of everyone. Long before Chamberlaine and Bartolozzi the need of publishing the drawings had been felt and dis- cussed. Lord Egmont in 1735 had pleaded with the Queen in the public interest;[11] but she pre- varicated, expressed fears for their safety, and said 'she did not love the public enough to have them spoilt.' Writing in 1762, Walpole again deplored that engravings were not available, and spoke of a first attempt by Vertue at fulfilling the task[12]. This scheme, however, was destined to fail, and Vertue, after spending 'part of three years on it,' during which he traced off on oiled paper as many as thirty-five of the portraits, broke off disconsolately for reasons unstated but easy to guess. Richard Dalton was the next to revive the project[13], and it so happened that his contribution to its fulfilment was, indirectly, to be an important one. Meeting Bartolozzi in Venice, in 1763, it was Dalton who prevailed upon him to come to England, with the ultimate result that is known to everyone. But Dalton's own attempts at rendering the drawings in line etching were very inadequate, and met with little response or commercial success. Ten plates had been issued in 1774[14], but not till 1792, the year in which Chamberlaine's enterprise began to materialize, did the number of his published plates increase to thirty-six[15]. To Bartolozzi's labours, on the other hand, both the publisher and public

as 'By H. Holbein,' not as is usual 'Drawn by H. Holbein.' Nos. 198-202, however, are captioned 'ditto,' and are all identifiable drawings. No. 100, which (again, perhaps not without significance) hung as a pendant to No. 102 (the item dated 1531), was a profile of Thomas Howard, Earl of Surrey (5 × ?¾ in.). This is very probably identical with a drawing (c. 5¾ × 4⅛ in.) now in the Morgan Library, New York, reproduced as plate 259 of the Fairfax Murray drawings publication. See below, p. 58, note on No. 83. The Morgan drawing is inscribed in the familiar roman lettering "Hen: Howard E: of Surrey," but it is clear that "Hen:" is an emendation, probably for "Tho:". It should be noted that the sitter was in fact Henry, not Thomas Howard. The drawing is stated to have been in the Arundel and Thane Collections (the latter no doubt Thomas Thane, 1782-1846, who specialized in *Arundeliana*). [8]*Life and Works of Hans Holbein*, 1867, pp.401-413. [9]A *terminus ante quem* is provided by the reference in Walpole's *Description of the villa . . . at Strawberry Hill*, 1774, p.59. At Strawberry Hill, incidentally, hung the Vertue copies about to be mentioned. [10]*Imitations of Original Drawings by Hans Holbein, in the Collection of His Majesty, for the Portraits of Illustrious Persons of the Court of Henry VIII.* The series includes 3 plates by C. Metz and 1 by C. Knight; 5 Portraits were omitted, viz., Nos. 2, 29, 30, 61 and 65 of the present catalogue. According to J. T. Smith in his *Book for a Rainy Day*, ed. 1845, pp.285/6, Metz was employed to engrave specimens for the projected work. [11]*Historical MSS. Commission: Report on the MSS. of the Earl of Egmont*, Vol. II (1923), p.210. [12]*Anecdotes of Painting*, ed. Dallaway-Wornum, 1862, Vol. I, p.86. [13]*Anecdotes of Painting*, ed. Dallaway- Wornum 1862, p.85 (note 3, contd.). [14]*The Court of Henry the Eighth . . . from Original Drawings in the Collection of His Majesty*, 1792. [15]A. Woltmann, *Holbein und seine Zeit*, ed. 1874, Vol. II, p.162.

FIG. I. CECILY HERON. ENGRAVING BY F. C. LEWIS AFTER THE DRAWING (NO. 5) AT WINDSOR

were nothing if not indulgent; for it can surely not have escaped the notice of either that his renderings of Holbein showed none of the felicity with which, in particular, he had interpreted Guercino.
It is said, indeed, that a plate by F. C. Lewis, that had been intended for inclusion in the work, was
suppressed by Chamberlaine to avoid embarrassment to the more famous engraver[1]. But whatever
its defects, Bartolozzi's series passed through a number of editions: à set of reduced copies in quarto
followed the first in 1812; then came a re-impression of the folio plates in 1828, and as late as 1884
they appeared once again as process reproductions. We need not here pause over various other
publications of later date and gradually improving quality, till we come, in 1911, to the series of
colour facsimiles edited by Professor Paul Ganz[2]. It includes the great majority, but not all, of the
plates subjoined, and far excels all other available reproductions of Holbein's drawings.

To complete the design of Chamberlaine's publication, biographical notices were compiled by
Edmund Lodge, Lancaster Herald. Unlike the plates, which are now entirely superseded, they
have retained much of their original value to this day, and there is no doubt that more recent
researches into the identity of the portraits owe much to Lodge's precedent and learning. The
basis, of course, for all such inquiry is the evidence provided by the inscriptions on the drawing
themselves, or to be more exact, by the inscriptions that appear on sixty-nine of the total of eighty-
five, the further sixteen having remained nameless. At this point we must revert to the Lumley
inventory of 1590[3], and complete the quotation of that vitally important entry with the further
information that the names were 'subscribed' to the drawings 'by Sir John Cheke, Secretary to King
Edward the 6.' One of the most learned men of his day, Cheke, then in his twenties, was summoned
to Court in July, 1542, to succeed Richard Cox as tutor to Prince Edward. On the newcomer's
arrival, therefore, Holbein himself was still on the scene, and the circle of his more recent sitters
still about him. That Cheke must have had personal contact with many of them is beyond doubt.
It follows that if the names now inscribed on the drawings correspond, as presumably they do,
with Cheke's identifications referred to in the inventory, they have abundant claim to interest and
attention, though not, of course, to blind belief. It is demonstrable that their accuracy is not in-
fallible, nor can the date of their recording have been otherwise than belated. But if, for instance,
certain members of the More family are misnamed, and others unnamed, this is less strange than
might appear at first, for these portraits are of an altogether earlier stage (1526/28). It is clearly for
his own contemporaries that Cheke's authority in general holds good. In any case it is well to allow
for some margin of error in the process of copying; for the present inscriptions are certainly not
his, nor even of his time, whatever Walpole may have thought on this point[4]. Writing of Tudor date,
apart from colour-notes and the like in Holbein's hand, occurs only twice. In neither case is that
writing Cheke's[5]. It would be idle to speculate in what form his information was originally 'subscribed,' whether on the drawings themselves (in which case it has been covered or cut away to the
last), on the pages of the book, or as a separate list attached to it. The present inscriptions fall into
two main groups, the more numerous by far being in roman lettering, while the few remaining
are in a detached cursive. In the case of six the name is, or was, inscribed in both styles; and in
one a longer inscription than usual, after opening on the normal roman pattern, concludes
in cursive. It has been suggested that the former type bears a significant resemblance to Hollar's
lettering[6], but whether really the inscriptions can be assigned, even vaguely, to the seventeenth

---

[1]A. B. Chamberlain, *op. cit.*, Vol. II, p.250. [2]*Les Dessins de Hans Holbein le Jeune* (Boissonas). [3]See above, p.9. [4]*Anecdotes of Painting*, ed. Dallaway-Wornum, 1862, Vol. I, p.85, note 3. [5]*Burlington Magazine*, Vol. LXVI (1935), p.223, note 5. [6]*Burlington Magazine*, Vol. LXVI (1935), p.223, note 5. The student concerned with this question must beware of forming an opinion from the inscriptions as they appear in the facsimiles, in general so sensitive, of Ganz's great publication. No doubt for technical reasons, the lettering seems to have been almost entirely re-written, with the result that its style appears considerably changed. Moreover, in No. 39, 'Iane' becomes 'Jane'; in 75, 'Sharinton' becomes 'Sherinton'; in 77, 'Carow.' becomes 'Carow', and so on.

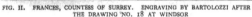

FIG. II. FRANCES, COUNTESS OF SURREY. ENGRAVING BY BARTOLOZZI AFTER
THE DRAWING NO. 18 AT WINDSOR

FIG. III. MODERN FORGERY OF A DRAWING RESEMBLING NO. 18 AT WINDSOR

century, is a very moot point. On the whole the most plausible assumption would seem to be that they originated at the time of the mutilation of the Great Booke.

The current belief that the cursive inscriptions mark a group of drawings added to the volume by Arundel[1] is purely hypothetical. It is not impossible that interpolations, more or less numerous, were actually made by him, and perhaps by other owners. But to single out the cursive group as such has little to recommend it ; and one is apt to find that such references as have been made concerning the subject of additions to the book, link up in some way with Walpole's confusion of the Holbein series with that other, less numerous, of French portraits in King Charles' Collection[2]. The Windsor series, as we now see it, certainly contains extraneous matter, but the only drawing definitely known to have been incorporated at a later date is the so-called *Amelia of Cleves*[3]. This joined its fellows in the eighteenth century, which is not to say that at an earlier stage it may not have formed part of the collection, but afterwards been detached from it. This converse problem, indeed, the problem of possible abstractions from the book, is in its way as interesting as the first. Since Holbein's English portrait studies, unlike the similar drawings of the Clouets[4], were certainly never intended for the sitters' retention, but solely for the artist's use when painting his pictures, they would not normally have come into circulation at all. It follows that such scattered examples as are found have, almost all, some semblance of deriving from the Whitehall residue, out of which the Great Booke was compiled. The Wilton drawing, that probable offshoot of the collection while on its fleeting passage through the hands of the Earl of Pembroke, calls for renewed

[1]P. Ganz, *Kritischer Katalog*, 1937, p.xv. [2]See above, p. 9, and compare, for instance, A. B. Chamberlain, *op. cit.*, Vol. II, p.248. [3]See R. N. Wornum, *Life and Works of Hans Holbein*, 1867, p.413; A. B. Chamberlain, *op. cit.*, Vol. II, p.183; P. Ganz, *Kritischer Katalog*, 1937, p.xv. [4]See L. Dimier, *Histoire de la Peinture de Portrait en France au XVIe Siècle*, Vol. I (1924), p,19.

attention in this context[1]. 'A few of the same sett,' to quote Walpole's phrase, that is presumably drawings thought or known by him to have been detached from the volume, were at one time in the possession of Lady Germain.[2] It is worth noting that three drawings, the so-called *Amelia of Cleves*, an unnamed lady in the British Museum, and the *Thomas Wriothesley* in the Louvre, share the common feature of being cut along their upper outlines. Another apparently cohesive group comprises the Dresden *Count Morette*, Lord Bradford's *Anne Boleyn*[3], and the anonymous gentleman at Berlin and has the characteristic of sloped corners. It would be wrong to stress the point unduly, but it can hardly be denied that these drawings together constitute evidence of a sort, and tend to show that abstractions from the book, not merely of single items, may have occurred.

Of the various topics that have still to be touched upon, that of the chronology of the drawings, their medium and method, and present-day state of preservation are, by their very nature, closely interconnected. The order as above indicates what is perhaps the most convenient line for approaching these problems. That the Windsor series as a whole cannot be said to lend itself to precise dating, is clear enough; but to fix at least an approximate date for each drawing, the criterion of style and technique is not alone available. In certain cases, for instance, the existence of dated pictures makes matters easy for establishing the studies with which they connect; and on occasion, too, a further method presents itself, a method obvious in principle though not without its pitfalls, that namely of deducing the date of the portrait from the sitter's age, when his or her identity and year of birth are known. But finally there is the evidence of fashion to be considered, which in the case of men shows itself in the cut of hair and presence or otherwise of beards, and in that of women more especially in the various styles of headdress worn. With both sexes a certain latitude from the dictates of fashion must be allowed for, but, particularly for the men, a fairly accurate line of demarcation can be drawn as between an earlier and a later style within the years of Holbein's residence in England. Thus, King Henry's edict of 1535, applying to all gentlemen of the royal household, provides a very useful point from which to work. 'On the 8th of May,' Stow writes in his *Annals*[4], 'the King commanded all about his Court to poll their heads, and to give them example, he caused his own head to be polled, and from thenceforth his beard to be notted and no more shaven.' Does the drawing of Simon George coincide with his first compliance with this royal behest, and the painting with its later fulfilment? Just as this change in the male appearance reflects a submission to the authority of France in matters of fashion, so also did the adoption by ladies of the close-fitting circular *crépine* or bonnet, in place of the peculiarly English style of gabled headdress, angular in its outline about the face, and with broad lappets falling behind or folded back over the crown. For a few years the two styles must have been almost equally in vogue, but by about 1540 the earlier seems to have been virtually supplanted by the other in all but exceptional cases.

In technique, the portrait studies of Holbein's first English period (1526/28) differ radically from the more numerous of his second visit (1532/43). In one respect especially this difference is very marked: from the 'thirties onwards the white surface of the paper was no longer allowed to show as such, but was invariably primed with a 'carnation or complexion of flesh colour'[5]. At the earlier stage, Holbein's method had been practically the same as that of the Clouets; drawing to a rather larger scale than in his later manner, he combined the use of black and coloured chalks

---

[1]See above, p. 10. [2]See the Advertisement (p.iii) of Vertue's *Catalogue of the Collection of . . . King James the Second*, 1758. [3]This drawing (Ganz 39), though unmarked, was, like the *Morette* (Fig. V), in Jonathan Richardson's Collection. Attached to a plumbago copy of it by Vertue in the Ashmolean Museum, is a picturesquely worded and somewhat malicious account in the younger Richardson's hand of how it passed into the possession of the third (?)Earl. [4]Quoted by A. B. Chamberlain, *op. cit.*, Vol. II, p.106, from ed. 1592, p.964, of *Annals of England*, with the obvious emendation of 'beard' for 'head.' [5]E. Norgate, *Miniatura*, ed. 1919, p.73.

FIG. IV.   HANS HOLBEIN :   A LADY, UNKNOWN (BRITISH MUSEUM)

FIG. V.   HANS HOLBEIN :   COUNT MORETTE (DRESDEN PRINT ROOM)

FIG. VI.   HANS HOLBEIN :   A GENTLEMAN, UNKNOWN (BERLIN PRINT ROOM)

on unprimed paper, the flesh-tones being rendered in sanguine. Whether the new method of priming the paper first engaged his attention before leaving London, during the intermediate Basel period (1528/32), or after his return, is not a matter of very great importance. So much is certain, that once having adopted the new technique early in the 'thirties, he never again relinquished it to go back to the other. Some change is noticeable in the primings themselves, for although they are applied, without exception, by the same wet process, there is a tendency as time goes on for stronger shades of pink to come into prominence. Here then we have yet a further aid to chronological classification, and one that is applicable within the last ten years of the artist's life, when comparatively little change in his actual style of draughtsmanship meets the eye. As between the first and second English periods, of course, a stylistic change, quite apart from the difference of method, is very pronounced. It cannot be overlooked how at the later stage the effect of plasticity decreased, and a greater simplification of form and concentration of expression came into being. Not infrequently in the later heads a few emphatic lines, drawn with the pen or brush, constitute virtually the aggregate of form and feature. But, for two reasons, we here already come upon controversial ground. This work with the pen or brush, is it really from Holbein's own hand and not of later addition? This abbreviation of form and decrease in plasticity, do they betray the use of a mechanical appliance which in his earlier work Holbein had not yet utilized?

That the Windsor series, generally speaking, is anything but well preserved, no practised eye could fail to detect. Being as they were, and what they are, the injury the drawings have suffered could hardly be otherwise. Of the various causes of damage to which such works are exposed, they combine in them the two most potent of all: frailty of medium and permanence of appeal. No medium is so liable to defacement as a dry, crumbling chalk; no work of art stands in greater danger of retouching than that which retains its hold on the attention of posterity, despite the passage of time and resulting damage. The Windsor Holbeins have suffered in both ways, from rubbing and reworking, and the fact has long been known and all too emphatically stressed. Norgate already described them as 'made worse by mending'[1]; adapting other phrases of his, Sanderson spoke of many 'in the book . . . spoyled by the injury of time and the ignorance of such as had it in custody'[2], Browne of their being the 'ruines of an admirable hand'[3]. Walpole was the first to formulate concisely the charge with which modern criticism has so abundantly concerned itself: that 'some have been rubbed and others traced over with a pen on the outlines by some unskilful hand'[4]. With varying degrees of improbability, Hollar[5], Vertue[6], and the younger Jonathan Richardson[7] have been named as the principal offender. Among present-day critics who have dealt with this question of retouching, the most recent and authoritative has gone the furthest length. Professor Paul Ganz, indeed, has clearly and categorically affirmed that in their pristine state the drawings were exclusively worked in chalks, and that in addition to restorations in their own medium, *all* the line-work which we now see done the pen or brush is false and of later date.

This sweeping doctrine, though rooted in an old tradition, and, moreover, to some extent anticipated among the moderns by such writers as Davies[8] and Glaser[9], this doctrine, nevertheless, came as an abrupt challenge to the general consensus of opinion among students. Nothing if not dogmatic in its presentment, it had one feature, and only one, of a persuasive kind, and that was implicit in the fact that in his earlier writings Ganz had himself held a different view. At that earlier stage he was ready to conform with a general trend of opinion which agreed in moderating rather

[1]E. Norgate, *Miniatura*, ed. 1919, p.74. [2]W. Sanderson, *Graphice*, 1658, p.79. [3]A. Browne, *Appendix to the Art of Painting in Miniature*, 1675, p.28. [4]*Anecdotes of Painting*, ed. Dallaway-Wornum, 1862, Vol. I, p.85, note 3. [5]Gerald Davies, *Hans Holbein the Younger*, 1903, p.123. [6]P. Ganz, *Kritischer Katalog*, 1937, p.xx. [7]F. Lugt, *Les Marques de Collections*, 1921, pp.403-4, No. 2170. [8]*Hans Holbein the Younger*, 1903, p.122. [9]Curt Glaser, *Hans Holbein d. J. Zeichnungen*, 1924, pp.21, 22.

FIG. VII.   HANS HOLBEIN :   SIMON GEORGE (FRANKFURT, STAEDELSCHES KUNSTINSTITUT)

than intensifying the strictures of the seventeenth century critics. For since 1867, when Wornum's important monograph appeared[1], a number of authoritative writers, including Woltmann[2], Schmid[3], and Stein[4] had investigated the condition of the drawings, and seen no reason to condemn it drastically. Not that the evident tendency among them could pass unnoticed to apologize for the frequence of hard and prominent contours. These are constantly being referred to, and a number of different explanations of this feature have been given in various places. For one, it has been suggested that the lines objected to, though by the artist himself, were more or less in the nature of subsequent corrections. Alternatively, their prominence has been accounted for by the partial effacement of the work in chalk, whereby a true balance of accent was disturbed. Yet another suggestion, and an important one in the present context, is that the undue emphasis on certain

[1]*Life and Works of Hans Holbein*, 1867, p.369. [2]A. Woltmann, *Holbein und seine Zeit*, 1874, Vol. II, p.162. [3]Thieme-Becker, *Künstler-Lexikon*, Vol. XVII (1924), p.348. [4]W. Stein, *Holbein*, 1929, pp.260-262, etc.

FIG. VIII. ALBRECHT DÜRER: AN ARTIST DRAWING A PORTRAIT WITH THE AID OF A TRACING APPARATUS (WOODCUT).

outlines resulted indirectly from the use of the tracing apparatus, that mechanical aid to which as yet only brief allusion has been made.

This appliance of which, it is suggested, Holbein availed himself for his later English portrait drawings, is of a very simple kind[1]. Essentially it consists merely of a pane of glass, fixed in a vertical position, and fitted at about arm's length with a peep-hole, the purpose of this latter being to prevent any displacement of the draughtsman's line of sight. By looking at his model through the peep-hole and pane, and with the use either of an oily pigment or crayon suitable for marking on glass, the draughtsman is able with little trouble to trace on to the pane the leading lines that he wishes to fix, these lines being afterwards transferred to paper and used as the foundation of a free-hand drawing. It is well known that in the sixteenth century this device was in frequent use. It was recommended by Leonardo for landscape drawing[2]. Dürer both described and illustrated it[3]. The first to suspect its use by Holbein was the eminent Viennese scholar, Joseph Meder[4], and though his opinion found no favour in the eyes of Ganz[5], it was duly endorsed by Glaser[6] and Stein[7].

Such mechanical intervention in the making of a work of art is apt to jar on modern suscepti-bilities, much in the same way as the use of photography. To many it will suggest an unfair practice, a makeshift to compensate for a lack of natural skill. In Dürer's comments casuistry and prejudice are strangely mingled, for while his general attitude remains contemptuous, he yet describes the

---

[1]R. J. Gettens and G. L. Stout in *Technical Studies*, July 1940, p.67, and *Painting Materials*, 1942, p.317. [2]*Leonardo Notebooks* II, pp.253/4; MS. 2038, Bibl. Nat. 24r. [3]*Unterweisung der Messung*, ed. 1538, fol. Q2. [4]J. Meder, *Die Hand-zeichnung*, 1919, p.467. [5]P. Ganz, *Kritischer Katalog*, 1937, p.xxi. [6]C. Glaser, *Hans Holbein d. J. Zeichnungen*, 1924, pp.20, 21. [7]W. Stein, *Holbein*, 1929, pp.159, 160.

appliance in minute detail, and commends its use without hesitation to the faltering artist, diffident of his unaided skill. How different is the attitude of W. R. Sickert. 'The camera,' he says, 'like alcohol or a cork jacket, may be an occasional servant to a draughtsman, which only he may use who can do without.'[1] That a juster estimate of such auxiliaries, their benefits and limitations, is here expressed, no one after due consideration is likely to deny. Nor to deny that Holbein, with his supreme mastery, could well 'do without,' and was free, if only for that reason, to apply any device that served his purpose. The question, in any case, that we are confronted with is not whether Holbein did well to adopt such a method, but whether in fact he did so.

It is unlikely that proof, either affirmative or negative, will ever be forthcoming. Certain conclusions, however, may reasonably be drawn after considering such factors as style, technique and treatment on the one hand, and of need and circumstance on the other. It is unfortunate that no preparatory studies have been preserved connecting with the portraits of members of the Steelyard, which figure prominently in Holbein's output during the early years after his return to London in 1532[2]. Such drawings must unquestionably have existed, and it would be interesting to know whether they already partook of the characteristics of his subsequent phase of activity, or whether possibly they approximated more nearly to the style of his first English period, when his fame was less, his time freer, and the disposition of his sitters perhaps not so exacting. It is a fact that the studies on primed paper, with relatively little plasticity and reinforced contours, and showing a marked simplification of form, a significant reduction of scale, and a certain uniformity of appearance due to what might be described as a 'photographic' quality, coincide in date with the period of his Court connexions, and are practically all of members of the Court circle. There must have been, for two reasons, a need for haste. With growing fame his commissions multiplied, and these were no longer the commissions of friends and compatriots whose patience in the wearisome task of sitting he could more readily tax. It is obvious that under these circumstances the tracing apparatus would be useful to him. Both for the harassed artist and his perhaps restless sitter, would it not be good to know that, with little time available, the leading lines and true proportions of the portrait had from the very outset been fixed? On the score of probability, therefore, there is much in favour of Meder's conjecture. And are not the very style, substance and appearance of the drawings such as to lend support to it? It is true, of course, that if really the draughtsman employed this method—a method, one would suppose, more likely to deaden than to stimulate his artistry,—the transcendent quality of the drawings themselves is nothing short of miraculous. But apart from this impress of genius that they so manifestly bear, is it not so that their every characteristic is such as to confirm and force home the correctness of the assumption?

Of the various points above enumerated, it is perhaps the decrease of plastic effect—surely not merely a *loss* of such effect, brought about as the result of rubbing—that in particular may need explanation. It is not perhaps generally realized that the visual image of normal sight, that is of sight with both eyes, differs essentially from the impression recorded on a single retina. In one-eyed seeing the forms appear flattened and summarized; they lose the stereoscopic effect as registered by normal sight, when an image is produced by the coordination of two views from slightly different angles, and when the seer, as it were, envelops the object with his gaze. It will be remembered that an integral part of the tracing apparatus is that peep-hole by which the line of sight of the draughtsman is fixed. What he sees through it and outlines on the pane is, therefore, the flattened and simplified image of which we have just spoken, and it becomes evident after brief reflection that even if only

---

[1]R. Emmons, *Life and Opinions of W. R. Sickert*, 1941, p.201. [2]The Berlin drawing, Fig. VI, is thought by P. Ganz (No. 90) to be of a German merchant, but there is no connexion with a known picture, and the point remains conjectural.

the preliminary groundwork of a drawing has been so laid in, the characteristics of one-eyed seeing are in some measure to be expected.

The next question to be considered is whether any traces remain which might betray one or other of the artist's alternatives for transferring his auxiliary sketch on the pane of glass to the paper. At this point a feature of our drawings must be mentioned, a very arresting feature, indeed, when once it has been observed: the prevalence of left-handed shading, that is of oblique strokes running downwards from left to right, as opposed to the normal right-to-left incline which comes naturally to everyone who draws with his right hand. The student acquainted with the problems attaching more especially to eighteenth-century drawings will be quick to grasp the implication. He will know that in the case of certain draughtsmen, such as Fragonard or Hubert Robert, offsets, or counterproofs, of chalk drawings are of frequent occurrence, and he will be aware of the importance of watching for left-to-right shading, since in many cases it betrays an offset more readily and reliably than any other feature. Now, among the later Windsor Holbeins there are passages here and there which, in their present condition, show something of the blurred effect common in offsets; and occurring, as they do, in conjunction with left-handed shading, one might well be tempted to suppose that offsetting played some part in Holbein's method of work, presumably at the stage of transferring the auxiliary sketch. It is not impossible, indeed, that such was the case. But on pursuing this matter of left-handed shading, one finds, once it is attentively watched for, that it appears everywhere and at all times in Holbein's drawings, and equally so in the case of silverpoint and other such media, which obviously preclude the possibility of offsetting. The fact, of course, is that Holbein was left-handed, and Carel van Mander, who duly recorded this in his *Schilderboeck* of 1604[1], was mistaken only in saying that it is nowhere to be detected. So far as our Windsor studies are concerned, therefore, what would normally seem indicative of an offset foundation must in reality be one of two things: direct left-handed shading, blurred perhaps, but nevertheless positive; or, alternatively, the impression produced by a process of indirect, or double offsetting.

Far-fetched and complicated as this process may sound, it is yet well within the bounds of what is practicable. Provided that a pigment of suitable consistency is taken, double offsetting presents no technical difficulty; and in the case of portrait drawings by so exact an artist as Holbein, its use, of course, would be far less surprising than that of offsetting in its simpler form. For could Holbein, of all men, ever have contented himself with rendering the right side of his sitter's face as the left, on the rough-and-ready assumption that they were virtually identical? But these remarks on the subject of double offsetting are not by any means intended to suggest that it was part of Holbein's normal usage. It is more with caution than with confidence that its relevance is here admitted at all. Indeed, from what has already been said of the present condition of the drawings, it should be abundantly clear that to express any really unqualified opinion as to the details of their method would be rash. It would be rasher still to assume that the artist always worked to the same formula. For divers reasons it seems highly probable that, when it served his purpose, he did not scorn to use the tracing apparatus. The next stage is more doubtful. But with the auxiliary sketch drawn on the pane of glass, its transfer by one method or another would necessarily have to be effected[2]. On occasion this may have been done by squeezing from a preliminary offset. Such passages, however, in the actual drawings as have somewhat the look of being offset in a tacky pigment, may in reality be just a much rubbed surface of black chalk, the original texture of which has been further

[1]See Constant van de Wall's translation of *Carel van Mander: Dutch and Flemish Painters*, 1936, p.93, and J. Meder, *Die Handzeichnung*, 1919, p.580. Walpole (*Anecdotes*, ed. 1862, p.74) denies the artist's left-handedness, but for a very ill-considered reason. [2]The relevant passage in Dürer's *Unterweisung der Messung* is not very informative: *verzeychen mit einem pensel ausz einem glaser lot auf das glas, darnach zeychen das selb auf das ding darauf du molen wilt* (ed. 1538, fol. Q2).

disguised by a belated application of fixative, or by touches with the brush and water. A method of transfer more likely to have been favoured is that of tracing to a sheet of oiled paper, and subsequent indentation of the lines so traced, the reverse of the tracing paper having been loaded with chalk. The characteristic appearance of line-work so transferred is not easy to define, but unless subsequently improved, it would show a certain insensitiveness and lack of continuity and accent. Among the Windsor drawings line-work of this nature unquestionably occurs, particularly in subsidiary passages such as the outlines of sleeves and headgear. But the factors of rubbing and reworking, of partial effacement and consequent strengthening, are ever present, and this makes definite conclusions more than ever difficult to reach, since, of course, a line deadened in the process of reinforcement by an unskilled hand might closely resemble the master's line, deadened by the process of transfer. Full of uncertainty as this question of transfer is, it seems safe to say that a primed paper would be helpful to either method, and also that the results obtained, whether by the one or other method, might well be such as to make it essential to re-draw the contours with a firm hand in order to give precise delineation and accent to the whole. Nor would it be surprising if these accents were distributed with a certain lack of balance. It must always be remembered that these drawings we are here concerned with were not intended to stand as independent works of art, but that their sole purpose was to provide the painter with the pattern he needed, and to enable him to proceed without constant reference to the living model.

If in this difficult and complex matter one statement may be made with full assurance, it is that the indiscriminate condemnation of *all* the penwork and brushwork oversteps its mark by a wide margin[1]. The theory is untenable on the evidence of the drawings themselves, even though the description of Holbein's technique as given by Norgate speaks only of the use of chalks. For what they are worth, Norgate's remarks (and they are certainly the remarks of a craftsman conversant with technical processes) fit in with Ganz's contention and give support to it. But let us not forget that it was nearly a century after Holbein's death that Norgate composed his treatise, nor omit to give full consideration to the evidence of the actual drawings themselves. These contradict the theory clearly and emphatically. There is penwork, for instance in *Godsalve* and *Lord Vaux*, which is of exquisite quality and sensitiveness; and the same is true of brushwork in others, such as *Ormonde* and *Lady Richmond*. Notes of colour and texture written with the pen or brush may again and again be observed, which are clearly of a piece with the drawings themselves, and which no would-be restorer, hoping to revive an almost obliterated sketch, could conceivably either have felt himself called upon to re-write, or have succeeded in so doing, especially in a language unfamiliar to him. But what is equally certain is that there is also penwork, and to a lesser degree brushwork, of a much inferior quality. Here the restorer's hand, making 'worse by mending,' will readily be conceded; and what could be more plausible than that he followed to the best of his ability the pattern of other drawings in the series, less effaced and better preserved precisely for the reason that they had been reinforced by the artist himself with pen or brush, and so had been rendered more durable? Whether it be for suspect passages in ink or chalk, in principle only one criterion is admissible to distinguish between what is original and what is not. The test of quality alone can decide, and this is admittedly not always an easy test to apply. The series as a whole abounds in problems, and a number of these undeniably remain unsolved, with little prospect that either time or the clarifying process of study will ever finally penetrate them.

                              *   *   *   *

---

[1] The same, incidentally, seems to be true of the penwork, generally condemned, occurring in the wonderful silverpoint portrait drawings by the artist's father, the elder Hans Holbein.

Hic frigent artes, petit Angliam ut corrodat aliquot Angelatos: writing to his friend Petrus Aegidius in Antwerp to inform him of Holbein's forthcoming journey to England, so did Erasmus explain its reason and state its purpose. At Basel the arts were indeed freezing; and the pun on Angles and angels (the unit of gold then current in England), a trite one perhaps, was nevertheless not ill-chosen to express the traveller's open intention of seeking fortune rather than fame. Holbein arrived in London for the first time about the month of October, 1526. Without, alas, having counted Wolsey among his sitters, he started back for home in the spring or early summer of 1528. An interval of four years at Basel does not here concern us. Before the end of 1532 he was back again in London. He died there, 'choked by pest,' between 7 October and 21 November, 1543. Within the narrow compass of these dates all the drawings by Holbein in the Royal Collection are contained,—a series infinitely revealing of at least one aspect of his genius, a page of history never more vividly told.

FIG. IX. HANS HOLBEIN : THE MORE FAMILY GROUP (BASEL, OFFENTLICHE KUNSTSAMMLUNG)

CATALOGUE

(For a list of bibliographical abbreviations and table of references, see below, p. 60)

Frontispiece

SOLOMON AND THE QUEEN OF SHEBA (12188). On vellum, $9 \times 7\frac{3}{16}$ in. (229 × 183 mm.): silverpoint; pen and brush in bistre and grey wash, heightened in white and gold, with touches of red and green water-colours (box of strawberries held by kneeling figure on right) and a background of turquoise blue. Inscribed REGINA SABA in the foreground to right of centre; and on either side of the throne (quoting II *Chronicles*, ix), BEATI VIRI TVI . . . . ET BEATI SERVI HI TVI / QVI ASSISTVNT CORAM TE . . . . OMNITPE ET AVDIVNT / SAPIENTIAM . . . . TVAM (in gold on blue); on the curtain behind Solomon, SIT DOMINVS DEVS TVVS BENEDICTVS, / CVI COMPLACIT IN TE, VT PONERET TE / SVPER THRONVM SVVM, VT ESSES REX / (CONSTITVTVS) DOMINO DEO TVO. (in black heightened with gold); and on the steps of the throne VICISTI FAMAM / VIRTVTIBVS TVIS (in black heightened with gold).

This drawing, or rather miniature painting, is not mentioned in the Royal inventory of 1542 as stated by P. Ganz (*Kritischer Katalog*, 1937, p. xiii), but it does occur, described as *Regina de Saba in miniatura chiaroscuro*, in the Arundel inventory of 1654 (see *Burlington Magazine*, XIX (1911), p. 286). It was etched by Wenceslas Hollar in 1642, while in the Arundel Collection (Parthey 74), and it may have been on that occasion that the page of vellum was marked off at regular intervals along its margins, as if for squaring. It is unlikely that the drawing was at any stage mounted in the Great Booke, but it decorated Queen Caroline's Closet at Kensington along with the portrait studies, and was listed by Vertue (No. 37). The engraved diagram of the 'Chimney side of the Closet' shows it to have been, unaccountably, in a circular frame, which explains why Walpole wrongly described it as a circular drawing. See *Anecdotes of Painting*, ed. Dallaway-Wornum, 1862, p. 85.

The resemblance of Solomon to Henry VIII, and the fact that he is bearded, fix the year 1535 as the earliest possible date of the drawing; but it is more probably a trifle later, when the artist's Court connexions had been more closely established. The obvious vein of flattery suggests that it was perhaps presented by the artist to the King. Whether it was conceived as a design for a mural decoration, like those carried out by Holbein for the Steelyard, remains conjectural. In style and composition it shows much resemblance with the copy, at Dresden, of a lost *Death of Virginia* (*Klassiker der Kunst*, p. 174).

(1-7).

STUDIES FOR THE MORE FAMILY GROUP

The picture, now lost, was probably ordered to commemorate Sir Thomas More's fiftieth birthday, and started soon after Holbein's arrival in England. A carefully drawn pen sketch of the whole composition, modi-fied at a later stage in but a few details, was conveyed by the artist to Erasmus and is now in the Basel Museum (Fig. IX). Copiously annotated in the hand of Nicholas Kratzer (see *Burlington Magazine*, Vol. LXXXIV (1944), p. 138) it gives the names and ages of all the sitters, from which its date may be inferred to be not later than 7 February, 1527. A copy of the lost picture, signed *Richardus Locky Fec. Ano. 1530*, is in the possession of Lord St. Oswald at Nostell Priory (see M. W. Brockwell, *Catalogue of the Pictures at Nostell Priory*, 1915, pp. 82 seq.). Various other copies with modifications and additional figures of later members of the family exist. For reproductions of these and a general discussion of the composition, see P. Ganz in *Festschrift zur Eröffnung des Kunstmuseums*, Basel, 1936, pp. 141-153. According to Van Mander, the original was a large canvas painted in distemper. It decorated a room in More's house in Chelsea, and, after his fall, was removed, passing into the hands of Andreas de Loo, later of Thomas More, the Chancellor's nephew, and then of Thomas Howard, Earl of Arundel. After the dispersal of the Arundel Collection it belonged to Franz and Bernard von Imstenraedt, and from them passed to Carl von Liechtenstein, Bishop of Olmutz, who also acquired Holbein's *Triumphs of Wealth and Poverty*, painted for the Steelyard. It may have perished in a fire in the Palace of Kremsier in 1752. See *Burlington Magazine*, Vol. LXXXIII (1943), p. 279; Vol. LXXXIV (1944), p. 129 and p. 134.

1. SIR JOHN MORE (12224).

On unprimed white paper, $13\frac{15}{16} \times 10\frac{7}{8}$ in. (354 × 276 mm.); chalks: black (hat, etc.), brown (fur collar), red (face), light yellow (hair). Eyes: grey-blue. Inscribed (tarnished gold and crimson) in left upper corner, **Iudge More Sʳ Tho: Mores Father.** Water-stains in various places.

Later retouching, in black chalk, seems to be restricted in the main to the parts about the shoulders. The drawing, like all the others of the series, both on primed and unprimed paper, shows intermittent pink lines skirting the edges of the page at a distance of about $\frac{1}{4}$ in. Applied with the brush in water-colour, they have (in the case of No. 32, for instance) sufficiently the appearance of an intentional border-line, to have been mis-described as such. Actually they seem to have been applied when the drawings were removed from their frames, with the purpose of touching out the marks left on their surface owing to contact with the edges of the glass or rabbet. The shade of colour, uniform throughout, is never otherwise than badly matched. The present study was closely followed for the face and hat both in the Basel drawing and the finished picture (third figure from left); but in the two latter the robe is unfaced and the fur collar omitted.

Sir John More, father of Sir Thomas More, born 1450/53; married Agnes Graunger, 1474; Butler of Lincoln's Inn and afterwards barrister; Serjeant-at-Law, 1503; Judge of the Common Pleas, 1518, and of the King's Bench, 1523; died 1530.

2. SIR THOMAS MORE (12225).

On unprimed white paper, $14\frac{15}{16} \times 10\frac{1}{8}$ in. (380 × 258 mm.): chalks: black, red (lips, touches in eyes, and stumped to produce a faint complexion over face); pale brown water-colour wash (hat). Inscribed *Sier Thomas Mooer*, above in centre, in a contemporary, but not characteristically English hand.

The wash is flat and uninteresting and certainly not from Holbein's hand. The contours of the face, eyes, mouth, etc., have also been re-worked. The general effect is empty, and even as a rapid and preliminary essay in portraiture, rubbed and retouched, the drawing is somewhat unconvincing. But it agrees essentially with the head of More in the Basel drawing (fifth figure from left) and presumably preceded it, also with the 1527 portrait of the H. C. Frick (formerly Huth) Collection (*Klassiker der Kunst*, p. 69). Its relation to the Nostell Priory picture seems less close. There is a slight suggestion of left-handedness in some of the lines of the fur collar.

Thomas More, Holbein's first patron in England, born 1477/78; entered New Inn, 1494, and Lincoln's Inn, 1496; Member of Parliament, 1504; published *Utopia*, 1516; Privy Councillor, 1518; knighted 1521; Speaker of the House of Commons, 1523; succeeded Wolsey as Lord Chancellor, 1529; resigned 1532; executed 1535; beatified 1886; canonized 1935.

3. SIR THOMAS MORE (12268).

On unprimed white paper, $15\frac{13}{16} \times 11\frac{13}{16}$ in. (402 × 301 mm.): chalks: black (hat, robe), brown (fur collar, hair), red (face, narrow vertical strip under chin), yellow (chain over right shoulder). Pricked for transfer. Inscribed (tarnished gold and crimson) near left upper corner **Tho : Moor Ld Chancelour.**

This is no doubt the study directly connected with the principal figure in the Family Group. Only the line of the chain differs. The face has a far greater depth of expression and subtlety of characterization than No. 2. Like the other, however, it is drawn to an almost life-size scale, and differs in that from all the other studies of this group. Apart from the Chatsworth cartoon fragment (*Klassiker der Kunst*, p. 180) connecting with the Royal Group in the Privy Chamber at Whitehall, it is the only known instance in Holbein's work of a drawing being pricked for transfer. The scale of the picture is thereby indicated, and the fact that the other studies are not pricked duly explained. Left-handed hatching is noticeable, particularly in the hat.

4. ELIZABETH DAUNCEY (12228).

On unprimed white paper, $14\frac{5}{8} \times 10\frac{5}{16}$ in. (371 × 262 mm.): chalks: black, brown (forehead rolls of headdress), yellow (rectangular outline of *décolletage*, chequered pat-

tern on side of headdress, etc), red (lips, a faint carnation over face and neck, and fainter under the transparent muslin at throat). Colour-note *rot* (red) in the artist's hand on dress. Erroneously inscribed (tarnished gold and red) in left upper corner **The Lady Barkley.** Water-stains on the lower part of the headdress.

The contours of the brow, nose and mouth in particular have been noticeably retouched. Left-handed shading is much in evidence. Study for the figure on the extreme left of the Basel drawing, and second from the left in the Nostell Priory copy of the picture. In both she is represented pulling on a glove.

Elizabeth, second daughter of Sir Thomas More, born 1506; married William, son of Sir John Dauncey, Knight of the Body to Henry VIII, 1525. The Lady Berkeley, wrongly named in the inscription, was Sir John Savage's daughter who, in 1533, married Thomas, Lord Berkeley, and died in 1564, aged 58. The two ladies were therefore the same age, which may to some extent explain the confusion between them.

5. CECILY HERON (12269).

On unprimed white paper, $15 \times 11\frac{1}{8}$ in. (384 × 283 mm.): chalks: black, yellow (rectangular outline of *décolletage*, stomacher, rim of pendant), brown (hair), red (centre of pendant, lips, and a faint carnation of the flesh parts).

The drawing has evidently suffered greatly by retouching, particularly the left eye, the outline of the veil falling to the right shoulder, and the projection of the headdress at the left cheek. The yellow chalk of the stomacher has evidently been worked upon in a wet process. The study connects with the third figure from right in the Family Group, where the position of the right arm, in conjunction with the general pose, betrays a reminiscence of Leonardo da Vinci's *Lady with the Ermine*, in the Czartoryski Museum at Cracow. See *Anzeiger für schweizerische Altertumskunde*, N.F., Vol. xxxviii (1936), pp. 31-39.

Cecily, third and youngest daughter of Sir Thomas More, born 1507; married Giles, son of Sir John Heron, Treasurer of the Chamber to Henry VIII, 1525; widowed in 1540 by the execution of her husband.

6. JOHN MORE THE YOUNGER (12226).

On unprimed white paper, $15\frac{1}{16} \times 11\frac{3}{16}$ in. (383 × 284 mm.): chalks: black, red (traces in face), brown water-colour wash (hair), and a faint carnation over the face and neck. Annotated by the artist *lipfarb brun* (complexion brown) in right upper corner. Inscribed (gold and scarlet) in left upper corner **Iohn More Sr Thomas Mores Son.**

The face is considerably damaged, particularly the right eye. Whether the washes are original is somewhat doubtful. Left-handed shading is throughout much in evidence, this feature, indeed, being perhaps more noticeable here than in any other of the drawings. The study is for sixth figure from left in the Family Group, but both in the Basel drawing and the Nostell Priory copy the figure, otherwise unchanged, is bareheaded.

John, only son of Sir Thomas More, born 1508; married Anne Cresacre, 1529; imprisoned about 1535, but later released; died before 1559. The tradition that he was feeble-minded is probably incorrect.

7. ANNE CRESACRE (12270).

On unprimed white paper, 14¾ × 10 9/16 in. (375 × 268 mm.): chalks: black, brown (hair), yellow (outline of *décolletage*, double band on headdress, etc.), red (lips and a faint carnation, (?) with wash, over face, neck and throat). Eyes: pale grey-blue.

Rather badly rubbed and probably somewhat reinforced. Study for the fourth figure from left in the Family Group. But while in the drawing the lady is seated, as is shown by the roughly sketched chair-back, the figure, visible only above the waist, is evidently intended, both in the Basel drawing and the Nostell Priory picture, to be standing. A hole in the right sleeve, about 3 in. from the lower margin, is one of many such injuries occurring in the series, sometimes two or more in the same sheet, and seems to indicate that the drawings were attached to the pages of the book by means of scattered dabs of adhesive which in the process of lifting produced tears.

Anne, daughter of Edward Cresacre of Barmbrough, Yorks., born 1512; betrothed to John More in or before 1527 and married to him, 1529; married secondly (according to P. Ganz), George Weste in 1559.

8. MARGARET GIGGS (12229).

On unprimed white paper, 15 3/16 × 10¾ in. (385 × 273 mm.): chalks: black, red (lips, a faint carnation over face and neck, and fainter under the transparent muslin at throat), brown (hair). Erroneously inscribed (gold and scarlet) near left upper corner **Mother Iak.**

Somewhat rubbed and damaged, particularly in the face. The eyes and end of the nose are noticeably retouched. The figure occurs on the extreme left of the Nostell Priory picture, the place occupied by Elizabeth Dauncey in the Basel drawing. Originally (that is, in the drawing) Margaret Clement was the second figure from left, and she was represented in a slightly stooping position, as if about to address a remark to Sir John More, and to draw his attention to a passage in the book which she is holding in her left hand. This more prominent figure was probably modified with the intention of subordinating it to that of More's daughter standing beside her. Hollar's etching, Parthey 1552, which is dated 1648 and inscribed *Holbein inu.* corresponds in reverse with the present study, but shows only the head and upper part of the body. Lodge refers to a picture in the collection of a Mrs. Hunter, now lost, said to resemble the drawing. Whether the etching is based on the drawing, or some such picture as that mentioned by Lodge, is a moot point. A similar fur cap with earflaps is worn by the lady with a squirrel and starling in Lady Cholmondeley's picture, repr. *Burlington Magazine*, Vol. XLVII (1925), p. 113.

The inscription on the drawing, demonstrably incorrect, refers to a Mistress Jack, or Jackson, who was nurse to the infant Prince Edward. Apart from all else, the style of the drawing is obviously of earlier date.

Margaret Giggs, a kinswoman and adopted daughter of Sir Thomas More, born 1508; educated in More's household by Dr. John Clement, afterwards Court Physician; married Clement, about 1530; present at More's execution, 1535; succoured the imprisoned Carthusians; went into exile and died at Mechlin, 1570.

9. A WOMAN: UNKNOWN (12217).

On unprimed white paper, 14 × 9¾ in. (356 × 248 mm.): chalks: black, red (lips, cheeks, and a faint carnation over the face and neck,? with wash). Eyes: light grey-brown.

Some of the outlines of the face and hat may have been lightly retouched, but apart from this, and some loss of definition due to rubbing, the drawing is well preserved. The subject seems to have been of the burgher class. Wornum's suggestion that she was German is less improbable than his alternative idea (followed by Holmes) that she was the woman known as Mother Jack, whose name is inscribed on the preceding drawing. Considerations of style and chronology are again incompatible with this assumption. It is pointed out by A. B. Chamberlain (*Hans Holbein the Younger*, 1913, Vol. II, p. 70) that the same style of headdress occurs on a small roundel, dated 1534, at Vienna (*Klassiker der Kunst*, p. 105). In spite of this the drawing must definitely be earlier.

FIG. X. HANS HOLBEIN : SIR HENRY GUILDFORD (WINDSOR CASTLE)

10. SIR HENRY GUILDFORD (12266).

On unprimed white paper, 15¼ × 10 15/16 in. (388 × 298 mm.): chalks: black (stumped or ? worked over with the brush in the hair), red (lips, eyelids; a brownish carnation over the face ? rendered with the brush with wash or water). Inscribed (tarnished gold and crimson) in left upper corner, **Harry Guldeford Knight.** Water-stains in many places.

Study for a picture (Fig. X) in the Royal Collection, Windsor Castle, commissioned, according to Ganz's conjecture, on the occasion of Guildford's elevation to the Order of the Garter. The picture is inscribed *Anno D: mccccccxxvii | Etatis. Suæ. xlix*, the latter indication conflicting with the recorded statement that Guildford in 1529 gave his age as 40. The counterpart of this portrait, representing the second Lady Guildford and likewise bearing the date MDXXVII, is in the Museum of St. Louis, U.S.A. A study for it, but in a more frontal pose, is at Basel (Fig. XI). On these portraits and their connexion, see *Festschrift zur Eröffnung der Kunstmuseums*, Basel, 1936, pp. 154/6. An old but indifferent copy of the present drawing, alleged to be in ' pen and wash on prepared red paper with the Basel

FIG. XI.   HANS HOLBEIN :   LADY GUILDFORD   (BASEL, ÖFFENTLICHE
KUNSTSAMMLUNG)

watermark, 420 by 250 mm.' was formerly in the J. P. Heseltine
Collection; see *Original Drawings chiefly of the German School in the
Collection of J.P.H.*, 1912, plate 23. The reference to an 'original
drawing' at Basel, quoted (p. 157) by C. H. Collins Baker, *Catalogue
of the Principal Pictures at Windsor Castle*, 1937, rests on a confusion.
Hollar's etching of 1647 (Parthey 1409) is not from the drawing.

Henry Guildford, son of Sir Richard Guildford, born (?)
1478/89; knighted, 1511/12; appointed Royal Standard
Bearer, 1513; Master of the Horse, 1515-1522; Comptroller of the Household, c. 1523-1530; Chamberlain of
the Exchequer, 1526; died 1532.

11. A WOMAN: UNKNOWN (12273).

On unprimed white paper, $15\frac{15}{16} \times 11\frac{1}{2}$ in. (405 × 292 mm.):
chalks: black, red (face). A somewhat yellowish carna-
tion, produced by the combined use of (?) stumped chalk
with brush and water, covers the face, neck and bosom,
and is graduated to suggest the transparency of the hood
adjoining its vertical outline on right, and of the muslin
on either side of the V-shaped *décolletage*. Annotated by
the artist *atless* (silk) near right lower corner, and *dam*
(damask) and (?) *rot* (red) below, near centre.

As in No. 6, left-handed shading is very prominent, and appears in
some of the passages of intensest black, which might otherwise be
mistaken for retouching. Actually the drawing, though no doubt
rubbed, and possibly reinforced a trifle about the eyes, chin and
mouth, is in fair condition. A picture is not known. The style is
clearly that of Holbein's first English period. In addition to the

evidence of watermarks, Ganz quotes in support of this the fact that
the notes of tissue are in German. Actually, though no English inscriptions are known to occur early, German inscriptions can equally
well be late; witness, for instance, Nos. 61 and 70.

12. WILLIAM WARHAM, ARCHBISHOP OF CANTERBURY (12272).

On unprimed white paper, $15\frac{3}{16} \times 12\frac{3}{16}$ in. (401 × 310
mm.): chalks: black (partly stumped), red (neckband,
touches in face), yellow and brown (fur). Inscribed (gold
and scarlet) in left upper corner, . . . : **Waramus Arch B**
Cant:

The general appearance of the drawing is tired and tampered. It has
certainly suffered considerably from rubbings and been reinforced
along its outlines, and otherwise reworked. Left-handed shading is
noticeable in the fur. The date is fixed as 1527 by an inscription
Anno Dm MDxxvij Etatis Sue LXX which occurs both on the smaller
(and preferable) version, at Lambeth, and the slightly larger, harder
and less harmonious version, in the Louvre (Fig. XII), of Warham's
portrait. See *Klassiker der Kunst*, pp. 70, 71. The latter version may be
in the nature of an autograph replica; for a fine old copy of the
Lambeth picture, see *Catalogue of Paintings at Ditchley*, 1908, p. 30,
No. 44 (repr.). The drawing is unequalled for its penetrating
characterization.

William Warham, born (?) 1450/56; Fellow of New College, Oxford, 1475; on missions to Rome and Flanders,
1490/91/93; Master of the Rolls, 1494-1502; Joint Envoy
to the Duke of Burgundy, 1496-99, and to the Emperor
1499, 1501/02; Bishop of London, 1502; Lord Chancellor, 1504-15; Archbishop of Canterbury, 1504; Chancellor of Oxford University, 1506-1532; in conflict with
Wolsey, 1518-23; died 1532.

FIG. XII.   HANS HOLBEIN :   REPLICA OF THE LAMBETH PORTRAIT OF
ARCHBISHOP WARHAM (LOUVRE)

FIG. XIII. CARDINAL FISHER, BISHOP OF ROCHESTER (BRITISH MUSEUM). COPY OF THE DRAWING, NO. 13, AT WINDSOR

13. CARDINAL FISHER, BISHOP OF ROCHESTER (12205).

On an opaque, dull-pinkish priming, $15\frac{1}{8} \times 9\frac{3}{16}$ in. (383×234 mm.): chalks: black, red (face); washed in brownish water-colour (cap), and reinforced with brush and (?) pen in indian ink (contours of face). Inscribed below with the pen in a contemporary italic hand, *Il Epyscop° de resester fo . . . . ato Il Cap° lan° 1535.*

One of the most historic drawings of the series, it is also one of the most damaged and problematical. It has been very much rubbed and reworked. The wash is clearly of later date, and the work in indian ink is also far from being of convincing authenticity. Note, however, the apparently left-handed slant of the brush strokes on the lappet of the cap on left. In spite of all, the expression of the face is much more penetrating and subtly characterized than that of the old copy, also on primed paper, in the British Museum (Fig. XIII), which has on occasion been claimed as genuine. Another copy, from the Percy and Heseltine Collections (repr. in *Original Drawings chiefly of the German School in the Collection of J.P.H.*, 1912, plate 22) is very feeble, and might derive from the British Museum version rather than the Windsor original.

It is not impossible that the date of the drawing is, as generally assumed, of about 1528. But around this statement in the various books is a welter of inaccuracy. Here are some relevant points: (1) To reconcile the technique with a date in Holbein's first English period, Ganz affirms that the priming of the paper was added later. Such a manipulation is altogether incredible. Further, he bases his assumption that the date is 1528 on the evidence (!) of an inscription on a *reproduction* of the drawing in St. John's College, Cambridge, which he quotes as follows: 'from Holbein's sketch made in the 59th year of the bishop's age and eight years before his martyrdom 1535.' Though not at present traceable, this reproduction can be nothing other than the frontispiece of T. E. Bridgett's *Life of Blessed John Fisher*, captioned as above on no better evidence than the author's computation (see third edition, 1902, p. 15). Eight years before 1535, incidentally, is 1527, not 1528. (2) In Thieme-Becker's *Kunstler-Lexikon* (Vol. XVII, p. 344), H. A. Schmid quotes A. B. Chamberlain's authority for the statement that a copy of the lost original painting for which the drawing served, again the property of St. John's College, Cambridge, is dated 1528. In fact, Chamberlain (I, p. 325) rightly quotes the Catalogue of the Tudor Exhibition (1890, No. 138) to the effect that the panel is inscribed *A° Ætatis 74*, and he wrongly adds that as Fisher was born in 1456 (!) the picture must in consequence (!) be of 1528. Like the aforesaid reproduction, the St. John's portrait is not at present to be found.

The Italian inscription, old, though certainly neither in Holbein's hand nor Cheke's, is obscured in meaning by the illegibility of the vital sixth word. Wornum reads *taiglato*; Woltmann, Chamberlain and F. F. Blackman (*Collegium Divi Johannis Evangelistae, 1511-1911* (1911), p. 59) read *tagliato*; T. E. Bridgett *tagilato*; Ganz *facolato* (for *fracassato*); A. J. Collins *stacchato*, Martin Davies *taculato*. Common to all these readings is that the past-participle is combined with *il capo* to signify '*was decapitated*.' But could that interpretation, so plausible on the face of it, nevertheless be incorrect? Could, perhaps, the verb be unconnected with *il capo*, leaving *Il capo lano 1535* to signify *New Year's Day 1535*? No special event in Fisher's life can be connected either with 25 March, 1535 or 1525, the latter alternative calling for consideration, as the 3 has much the appearance of being altered from a 2, the date indeed being rendered as 1525 in Bartolozzi's engraving.

If the drawing is of Holbein's first English period, the technique is anomalous; if it were of, say, 1532/33, it would be strange that the portrait should date from a time when the Bishop was already in Royal disgrace and under duress. Neither point is conclusive. The later dating has, on the whole, rather more in its favour from a stylistic point of view.

John Fisher, born ?1459/69; Master of Michaelhouse Cambridge, 1497; Vice-Chancellor, 1501; Lady Margaret Professor of Divinity, 1503; Chancellor of the University and Bishop of Rochester, 1504; opposed church reform, 1529; fined for denying validity of Royal divorce, 1534; imprisoned, attainted; beheaded, 22 June, 1535, soon after being raised to the purple; beatified, 1886; canonized, 1935.

14. MARGARET, LADY ELYOT (12204).

On a pink priming, $11 \times 8\frac{1}{4}$ in. (280×209 mm.): chalks: black, yellow (gable and lappets of headdress), red (lips, cheeks, etc., chequered pattern on gable), brown (over yellow on forehead rolls of headdress); heightened with body-colour (face) and reinforced in indian ink with pen and brush (contours of face, headdress, etc.). Inscribed (tarnished gold and crimson) in right upper corner **The Lady Eliot.**

For general remarks, see note to No. 15.

Margaret, daughter of John à Barrow (not, as stated by Lodge, Sir Maurice Abarrow), born about 1500;

married Thomas Elyot, about 1522; after his death in 1546, married Sir James Dyer, Chief Justice of the Court of Common Pleas; died 1569.

15. SIR THOMAS ELYOT (12203).

On a pink priming, $11\frac{1}{4} \times 8\frac{1}{8}$ in. (286×206 mm.): chalks: black, red (face), brown (fur at neck; hair, ? with wash), yellow (pendant cross; chain, with red outline near throat); heightened with body-colour (face) and reinforced in indian ink with pen and brush (contours of face, hat, hair). Inscribed (gold and scarlet) in left upper corner **Th: Eliott Knight.**

Nos. 14 and 15 are among the best preserved and most colourful of the series. They are clearly of an early date in Holbein's second English period, the appearance of the man in particular, with long hair and no beard, being typical of the older style of fashion. The treatment of the face shows analogy with that of Godsalve (No. 22); the penwork is subtle and delicate. Left-handed shading is prominent in both drawings. Pictures are not known.

Thomas Elyot, diplomatist, humanist and author of *A Boke called the Governour* (1531), born before 1490; Clerk of Assize, 1511-28; Clerk of the Privy Council, 1523-30; knighted 1530; twice Ambassador to Charles V, 1531/2, 1535; died 1546.

16. MARY, DUCHESS OF RICHMOND AND SOMERSET (12212).

On a pale pink priming, $10\frac{1}{2} \times 7\frac{15}{16}$ in. (267×201 mm.): chalks: black, brown (hair), red (lips), yellow (extremities of lines at collar), white (? kerchief); indian ink with brush (hat, plume). Annotated by the artist *samet rot* (velvet red), *schwarz felbet* (black velvet), and with the lady's initials MH and R (repeated). Inscribed (tarnished gold and crimson) in left upper corner **The Lady of Richmond.**

The face, modelled by delicate stumping, is considerably rubbed and shows traces of light retouching by a later hand along the eyelids and mouth. The brush work is most sensitive and masterly. The projecting extremity of the hat on left, the outline of the shoulders, and the rather obscure designs running horizontally across the lower part of the drawing, all show a somewhat mechanical quality which might be due to transference by indentation. The aforesaid designs are interpreted by Woltmann, probably rightly, as alternative renderings of the hat which was to be powdered over with the initials R (Richmond) or M H (Mary Howard). It is not impossible, however, that they signify that the dress was to have a horizontal panel of embroidery across the front. Both the headdress and costume seem to be of an unusual type. The indication *red* velvet is significant in relation to the early date, 1536, of the sitter's widowhood. A picture is not known.

Mary Howard, daughter of Thomas, third Duke of Norfolk, and sister of Henry Howard, Earl of Surrey, born 1519; married Henry Fitzroy, Duke of Richmond, natural son of Henry VIII by Elizabeth Blount, in or after 1533; died 1557.

17. HENRY HOWARD, EARL OF SURREY (12215).

On a pale pink priming, $9\frac{7}{8} \times 8\frac{1}{16}$ in. (251×205 mm.): chalks: black (partly stumped), red (cheeks, lips, etc.), brown (eyebrows, nose); reinforced with the pen in indian ink (contours of eyes, nostrils, mouth); washed with brown water-colour (hair). Inscribed (gold and scarlet) in left upper corner **Thomas Earl of Surry.** To left of the face a hole of considerable size; see above, No. 7.

The general condition of the drawing is good. There is probably a little later retouching in black chalk, but the penwork and wash are certainly original. A picture is not known. Though Lodge accepted the accuracy of the inscription and identified Nos. 18 and 17 as mother and son respectively, it was conclusively shown by Woltmann, A. B. Chamberlain (II, pp. 200/1) and Ganz, that the subject of the drawing must be Henry, not Thomas, Earl of Surrey. Thomas Howard, eighth Duke of Norfolk (1524) and Earl of Surrey (1513/14), was born in 1473 and is the subject of Holbein's picture of 1538/39 at Windsor (*Klassiker der Kunst*, p. 123). He was succeeded by Thomas, his grandson (born 1537/38) in 1554.

Sir Henry Howard, styled Earl of Surrey, eldest son and heir apparent of the eighth Duke of Norfolk, born 1516/18; proposed as husband for Princess Mary; Knight of the Garter 1541; wounded at Montreuil, 1544; Commander of Boulogne, 1545-46; superseded after a defeat at St. Etienne, 1546; executed, 1546/47. His poems, for which he is best remembered and linked in fame with Thomas Wyatt (below, No. 64), were printed, 1557, in Tottel's *Miscellany*. For dating the drawing it is well to remember that from October, 1532, to September, 1533, Howard was residing in France, though in June he returned to participate at the Coronation of Anne Boleyn.

18. FRANCES, COUNTESS OF SURREY (12214).

On a pink priming, $12\frac{3}{8} \times 9\frac{3}{8}$ in. (315×213 mm.): chalks: black, yellow (headdress, pendant, girdle), brown (eyes; over yellow on forehead rolls of headdress), red (lips, cheeks, touches in pendant and headdress); reinforced with the pen in indian ink (eyebrows, eyes, nostrils, mouth); heightened with body-colour (eyes, nose). Annotated by the artist *rosa felbet* (rose velvet) on the corsage and *felbet* . . . . on right sleeve. Inscribed (tarnished gold and crimson) in left upper corner **The Lady Surry.** above the right shoulder are traces of a deleted italic inscription of which *Surry* is still legible.

The condition of the drawing is on the whole good. The black fall of the headdress may be reworked, but the extremity projecting on left, also some of the contours of the sleeves and corsage, have much the appearance of lines mechanically transferred by indentation. A picture is not known. Ganz refers to a miniature, formerly in the Hawkins Collection, said to represent the Countess at the age of 23; but it is unlikely that she was as old when the present drawing, probably of about 1535, was made.

Frances (de Veer), daughter of John, fifteenth Earl of Oxford, born 1517; married Henry Howard, Earl of Surrey, 1532; widowed, 1546/47; married Thomas Steynings, before 1553; died 1577.

19. LADY RATCLIFFE (12236).

On a pale pink priming, $11\frac{13}{16} \times 8$ in. (301×203 mm.): chalks: black, red (lips, cheeks; with yellow in chain and headdress), brown (forehead rolls of headdress), yellow (crown of headdress, pattern on gable, chain); pen and indian ink (eyebrows, eyes, nose, mouth); brush and ink (stripes on rolls); metal point (detail of ornament on left, nearest shoulder). Annotated by the artist *damast black* on corsage, and *schwarz felbat* (black velvet) on left sleeve. Inscribed (gold and crimson) in left upper corner **The Lady Ratclif.** A water-stain on right.

Condition fair, but no doubt rubbed and to some extent reinforced. A picture is not known. Observe (below the sketches of ornament on left) lines seeming to represent a cushion at the lady's back, and compare the detail of hands in No. 21.

The sitter's identity is very uncertain, and the problem is only complicated by the occurrence, hitherto unheeded, of the letter S (reversed presumably for symmetry) among the details of ornament. Sir Robert Ratcliffe (1483-1542) was created Earl of Sussex in 1529. He was three times married, and his third wife, Mary, daughter of Sir John Arundell, might perhaps be represented. But one of his daughters-in-law would, on the evidence of the inscription (not, however, of the letter S in the detail) have a stronger claim to consideration. Henry Ratcliffe (1506-1557), who succeeded to the Earldom in 1542, married (before 1524) Lady Elizabeth Howard, daughter of Thomas, Duke of Norfolk. The apparent connexion of the drawing with Nos. 16-18 could perhaps be looked upon as supporting the belief that the last-named lady is represented.

20. JANE, LADY LISTER (12219).

On a pink priming, $11\frac{7}{16} \times 8\frac{1}{4}$ in. (290×210 mm.): chalks: black (partly stumped), red (lips, cheeks), yellowish-brown (forehead rolls of headdress), yellow (outline of gable on right); reinforced with the pen in indian ink (eyebrows, nose, mouth, contours of face, details in headdress). Eyes: bluish grey. Inscribed (gold and scarlet) near the upper margin **The Lady . . . . Lister.**

In fair condition. Left-handed shading is plainly visible in the headdress and right sleeve. The black chalk may have been somewhat strengthened, however; the penwork is of medium quality. A picture is not known.

Jane, daughter of Ralph Shirley, a lesser official at the Court of Henry VII, was, according to Lodge, first married to Sir John Dawtrey. After 1520 she married as her second husband Sir Richard Lister, who, after being Attorney General, Chief Baron of the Exchequer, etc., became, in 1546, Lord Chief Justice, and died in 1552, his wife surviving him.

21. JOAN, LADY MEUTAS (12222).

On a pale pink priming, $11\frac{1}{8} \times 8\frac{5}{10}$ in. (283×212 mm.): chalks: black (stumped for modelling of face, throat, etc.), red (face), yellow (forehead rolls of headdress, ? with wash; chain). A colour note (?) *Gl* (for gold) referring to the stripes on the rolls, appears on the folded veil of the headdress on right. Inscribed (gold and crimson) in left upper corner **The Lady Meutas.**

The drawing is rubbed, but it is doubtful whether it shows any appreciable degree of retouching. Again there are lines suggestive of transfer by indentation. A picture is not known. The sketch on right is referred to by Ganz as a detail for the costume and chain, but it is clearly meant for two hands, loosely interlocked, with rings on the fingers. The oval medallion has been shown by Ganz to connect with three jewellery designs, at Basel, representing the *Penitent Magdalen* (Ganz, 292-4). Marking the centre stone of the pendant, also one of the rings of the detail sketch, is a diminutive heart-shaped leaf, a symbol used by the Swiss and German designers for stained glass to denote the colour green, or, in this case, an emerald. The colour-note here tentatively read as *Gl* must also be somewhat in the nature of a conventional sign or flourish. It occurs fairly frequently (see Nos. 24, 57, 58, 60, 61), and in particular also Ganz 23), but it cannot be said that its interpretation is really conclusive, and the alternative *Sch* in Gothic script (? for *schwarz*, black) should be borne in mind.

The sitter is identified by Lodge as Joan (Ashley), wife of Sir Peter Meutas, 'a person considerably favoured by Henry the VIII,' of Norman descent and the owner of estates in Essex.

22. SIR JOHN GODSALVE (12265).

On a pink priming, $14\frac{7}{16} \times 11\frac{11}{16}$ in. $(367 \times 296$ mm.): chalks: black (traces), red (lips, cheek); point of the brush and indian ink (hair, eyebrows, shading of hands, contours, etc.); pen and indian ink (eyes, mouth); water-colour and body-colour: black (hat, gown), brown (fur facing of gown), greyish mauve (under-garment), turquoise blue (background), yellow (hat badge); white body-colour (shirt, cuffs, letter, whites of eyes). Inscribed (tarnished gold) in left upper corner **Sr Iohn Godsalue**, and below it, at the level of the ear, **S John Godsalue.**

Contrary to the opinion that the drawing, originally in chalks alone, is, as we now see it, entirely reworked, it may confidently be affirmed that, like the Basel portrait of Edward, Prince of Wales (Ganz 48), it is in all essential respects in its original state. The brushwork of the face is of conspicuous quality. A picture based on this design is not known, but the drawing must be studied in relation to the Dresden picture of 1528 (*Klassiker der Kunst*, p. 74), showing John Godsalve, with Thomas, his father (claiming to be aged only 47¹); also to a single portrait of John Godsalve, now in the Johnson Collection, Philadelphia, attributed by P. Ganz to Holbein (*Burlington Magazine*, Vol. xxvi (1914), p. 47), and dated by him about 1532-34, some 'two or three years' earlier than the drawing. Actually, though the subject of the drawing seems somewhat older than in the Dresden picture, no appreciable difference of age is visible as compared with the other, far from convincing picture. From a description it would seem that the colours of the dress correspond. Ganz, very plausibly, explains the renewed contact between Holbein and Godsalve by the fact that in 1532 the latter had connexions with the Steelyard.

John Godsalve, born about 1510; Clerk of the King's Signet, 1530; appointed to the Office of Common Meter of Precious Tissues, 1532; present at the operations at Boulogne, 1544; knighted 1547; Comptroller of the Mint, 1550; died 1556.

23. THOMAS BOLEYN, EARL OF WILTSHIRE (?) (12263).

On a pale pink priming, $15\frac{15}{16} \times 11\frac{9}{16}$ in. $(405 \times 294$ mm.):

chalks: black (lines in beard), red (traces in face); indian ink with pen (hair, eye-lashes, etc.) and brush (gown, hand); water-colours: red, (hat), light brown (with point of brush, beard); greyish blue (eyes); white body-colour (undergarment at neck, slashes of gown). Inscribed (gold and red) above in centre **Ormond.**

As in the case of No. 22, Ganz contends that the drawing is completely overworked, and distinguishes the hands of two retouchers. Though the rendering of the beard is rather over-meticulous, and the hat somewhat mechanical and uninteresting, the drawing of the gown shows a masterly breadth of treatment, and confirms the opinion that in the main the original state has not been modified. Some of the brush lines at the shoulders have been traced over with the pen and spoilt. A picture is not known. Probable date: about 1535.

Sir Thomas Boleyn, father of Queen Anne Boleyn, born 1477; Keeper of Exchange at Calais, 1509; Joint Constable of Norwich Castle, 1512; Treasurer of the Household, 1522; created Viscount Rochford, 1525, and Earl of Wiltshire and Ormonde, 1529; Lord Privy Seal, 1530; died 1539.

Lodge explains the inscription *Ormond* by pointing out that this Earldom was entailed on its bearer's heirs general, and that after the execution of Thomas Boleyn's only son, Lord Rochford, in 1536, it is not impossible that he would have used the title of Ormonde, which was to descend to his surviving daughter, in preference to that of Wiltshire. But the age of the sitter makes it extremely doubtful whether the identification is correct at all. W. Stein's suggestion (*Holbein*, 1929, pp. 273/4) that we have here George, the brother of Anne Boleyn, whose alleged incestuous relations brought both to the scaffold, is completely unsupported.

24. THOMAS, LORD VAUX (12245).

On a pale pink priming, $11 \times 11\frac{5}{8}$ in. $(279 \times 295$ mm.): chalks: black, brown (beard, moustaches), red (lips); metal point (gown); white body-colour (shirt), yellow (touches on hat at right extremity); reinforced in indian ink with the pen (hair, beard, embroidery on collar) and brush (hat). Annotated by the artist *silbe* (silver, twice), *rot* (red), *w. sam* (for *weiss sammet*, white velvet)? *Gl* (gold) . . . . *karmin* (. . . . carmine). An inscription (tarnished gold and crimson), probably **The Lord Vaux**, was in the upper left corner, but only the last two letters remain as the drawing has been cut to an irregular shape.

The technique is unusually elaborate. The hat, face, hair, beard and collar are rendered with great detail and sensitiveness. This part of the drawing is in good condition, but the gown may be to some extent reworked. Left-handed shading, much rubbed, is noticeable in the right sleeve. The cutting of the upper corners which mutilates the inscription must be of a relatively late period.

Thomas, second Baron Vaux of Harrowden, poet, born 1510; succeeded to title 1523; travelled to France in 1527 and 1532, with Wolsey and Henry VIII respectively; Captain of the Isle of Jersey till 1336; died 1556; posthumous publication of verses in Tottel's *Miscellany*, 1557.

25. ELIZABETH, LADY VAUX (12247)

On a pale pink priming, $11\frac{1}{16} \times 8\frac{1}{2}$ in. $(281 \times 215$ mm.):

chalks: black, red (face), yellowish brown (forehead rolls of headdress); metal-point (necklace, contours of dress); reinforced in indian ink with the pen (contours of face) and brush (veil of headdress, stripes on rolls); heightened with white body-colour (eyes, face, pearls on head-dress). Inscribed (gold and scarlet) in left upper corner **The Lady Vaux.**

The drawing seems to have suffered considerably from retouching. The indian ink wash in the headdress, though perhaps not so clumsy as in No. 26, is yet decidedly unconvincing. The penwork, too, is inclined to be insensitive, and the outlines in metal-point are drawn, as if for transfer to the panel, sharply and incisively. It should be noted, however, that there is no trace of chalk under the present lines of the necklace which correspond closely with the picture (see below) at Prague. The black chalk foundation of the figure is badly rubbed, but left-handed shading is still perceptible.

Holbein's original painting seems not to be preserved; but two versions of it, at Prague and in the Royal Collection at Hampton Court (*Klassiker der Kunst*, pp. 220, 221), both have documentary value. Lady Vaux is there represented with a carnation in her right hand, the left resting on her lap, a large circular medallion at her bosom, and ermine over-sleeves to her dress.

Elizabeth, daughter of Sir Thomas Cheney by his second wife, born (?) 1505/15; wife of Thomas, second Lord Vaux.

26. MARY, LADY HEVENINGHAM (?) (12227).

On a pale pink priming, 11 15/16 × 8 5/16 in. (303 × 211 mm.): chalks: black, yellow (gable and lappets of headdress, pendant, medallion), brown (forehead rolls of head-dress); reinforced in indian ink with the pen (eyebrows, contours of face, etc.) and washed in indian ink (veil of headdress, outline of *décolletage*); heightened with white body-colour (narrow band on gable, corsage at shoulders). Inscribed (gold and scarlet) in left upper corner **The Lady Henegham.**

That the drawing has been badly rubbed and reworked, in the face and elsewhere, is clear, nor can it be doubted that the heavy black surfaces of the fall, lacking all gradation and subtlety, have been daubed over. For contrast they should be compared with the work of a similar kind, but immeasurably superior quality, in, for instance, No. 16. The outline of the *décolletage* is considerably better than the veil and might be original. Left-handed shading, much rubbed, is noticeable in the sleeves. A picture is not known.

Like the unknown lady in the British Museum (Fig.IV; Vasari Society, I, 31), the present subject shows a certain resemblance to Margaret Roper in the More Family Group (Fig. IX). Both draw-ings, however, are definitely of later date, and the resemblance is probably accidental. Lady Heveningham's identity is obscure. Lodge supposed her to be Mary (died about 1563), daughter of Sir John Shelton and second wife of Sir Anthony Heveningham (died 1558). He dates the marriage as late as 1546, or little before. By her second marriage Mary Shelton became the wife of Philip Appleyard. Ganz casts doubt on Lodge's identification and suggests that the lady was Sir Anthony Heveningham's mother, herself a member of the Shelton family.

27. A LADY : UNKNOWN (12257).

On a rose pink priming, 10⅞ × 8 1/16 in. (276 × 204 mm.): chalks: black, red (touches in face, medallion at throat), yellow (with red, vertical outlines of bodice), yellowish-brown (forehead rolls of headdress); reinforced with the pen in indian ink (face, details of decoration on gable of headdress). Eyes: blue-grey.

The drawing is painfully disfigured by rubbing and retouching. The veil on left has obviously been worked over, and nearly all the pen-work is niggling and unworthy of Holbein. The details of embroidered ornament on the headdress suggest a better hand.

Hollar's etching of 1647, Parthey 1549, shows the figure in reverse enclosed in a circle (*Klassiker der Kunst*, p. 199). There is no justifica-tion either in Parthey's identification of the sitter as Catherine of Aragon, nor that as Lady Lister (see No. 20), to which he refers.

28. MARGARET, MARCHIONESS OF DORSET (12209).

On a pink priming, 13⅛ × 9⅜ in. (333 × 238 mm.): chalks: black, red (face, throat), dark brown (forehead rolls of headdress); reinforced with the pen in indian ink (con-tours of face, eyes, etc.) and with a hard metal.point (outlines of dress, hands, etc.). Inscribed (gold and scarlet) along the upper margin, **The Lady Marchioness . . . . of Dorset.** At various places on the right side of the drawing are traces of what appears to be accidental off-setting on to the pink prepared surface: in the right upper corner, for instance, cutting across the gable of the head-dress, outlines resembling the heraldic device of a *tree couped*.

That the drawing has been a most entirely spoiled by rubbing, the process of transfer to the panel (?), and reworking, is obvious. The original is now practically effaced, but traces of left-handed shading in the headdress proclaim it reliably to have been by Holbein in the first place. An original picture is not known, but a copy, correspond-ing in design with the drawing, is No. 496 of R. W. Goulding's and C. K. Adams' *Catalogue of Pictures belonging to the Duke of Portland* (1936, p. 197). A later copy is at Enville Hall. There are two small circular miniatures of Holbein's time, but not his workmanship: one in the Buccleuch Collection (B.F.A.C.: *Early English Portraiture*, 1909, p. 118, plate XXXIII; also C. Holme and H. A. Kennedy, *Early English Portrait Miniatures*, 1917, plate VII); the other in the Vienna Museum (*Burlington Magazine*, Vol. XLI (1922), plate facing p. 194). The background is blue, against which the dress appears black with ermine sleeves.

The sitter was identified by Lodge as Frances, Marchioness of Dorset (born 1517), mother of Lady Jane Grey. Actually she was the mother-in-law of Frances: Margaret, daughter of Sir Robert Wotton. She married, first, William Medley, and secondly, in 1509, Thomas Grey, second Marquess of Dorset of the second creation, Knight of the Bath and Garter (1477-1530; see D.N.B., Vol. XXIII, p. 202). The Marchioness died in 1535.

29. HENRY HOWARD, EARL OF SURREY (12216).

On a pale pink priming, 11 7/16 × 8¼ in. (290 × 210 mm.): chalks: black, red (face), brown (eyes, hair); reinforced with the pen in indian ink. Inscribed (gold and scarlet) in left upper corner **Tho: Earle of Surry.**

Though very much rubbed and injured by retouching, the drawing seems originally to have been genuine. With what a lack of under-standing the restorer went to work is shown by the hair which has now somewhat the appearance of being covered by a kerchief. (Chamberlain, II, p. 201, speaks of a skull-cap.) There can be little doubt that this portrait was in fact more or less contemporaneous with No. 17, and showed the same style of hairdressing with a fringe coming low over the forehead and the ears partly covered. The face is unmistakably the same, though perhaps a trifle older, and Ganz, who assigns the drawing to the second half of the sixteenth century, is certainly mistaken in suggesting that it represents Henry's son, Thomas Howard (1537/8-1572).

30. THOMAS, LORD VAUX (12246).

On a pale pink priming, $11\frac{7}{16} \times 8\frac{1}{8}$ in. (291 × 206 mm.): chalks: black, red (face), brown (beard). Eyes: pale grey-blue. Inscribed (tarnished gold and crimson) in left upper corner **The Lord Vaux.**

The drawing has been very badly rubbed and noticeably reworked. There are traces, nevertheless, of left-handed shading in the hat. Though Ganz considers it either the work of a follower of Holbein or a copy of a lost original, there is nothing in its appearance inconsistent with a much injured drawing by the master himself. The comparatively unscathed passage of the ear is finely drawn. Though Woltmann does not consider the resemblance with No. 24 to be entirely convincing, there can be no sort of doubt that the subject was in fact the same, at a rather later date, and after "polling" his head in accordance with the Royal edict of 1535. Though it is generally assumed that Nos. 24 and 25 constitute a pair, it is seriously to be considered whether No. 30 should not in fact replace No. 24, in which case the discrepancy in the direction of the eyes as between the two supposedly connected portraits would be removed.

31. WILLIAM RESKIMER (12237).

On a pink priming, $11\frac{9}{16} \times 8\frac{3}{8}$ in. (293 × 212 mm.): chalks: black, red (face, touches in beard), brown (hair, fur at collar), brownish-yellow (beard), white (highlights in face, collar). Eyes: grey-blue. Inscribed (gold and scarlet) about an inch from the upper border

FIG. XIV.   HANS HOLBEIN :   WILLIAM RESKIMER (HAMPTON COURT)

Reskemeer a Cornish . . . Gent:. There is a patched hole at the left temple. A rectangle, about $8 \times 6\frac{1}{2}$ in., is faintly perceptible (as if showing through from the back), enclosing the face and beard and cutting across the brow.

Well preserved on the whole, but with some niggling, no doubt later lines (e.g. back of head and nape of neck). Observe also the original left-handed shading of the coat on right as opposed to the darker, probably retouched passages below and to left of the beard. The drawing connects with a picture at Hampton Court (Fig.XIV). Like the portraits of Guildford, of 1527, and of Derrik Born, of 1533, the Reskimer picture shows a sprig of leaves in the background. It must be of a rather early date in Holbein's second English period.

The identification of the sitter as the younger son of John Reskimer (died 1504/5) cannot be accounted a certainty, but is probably correct. The elder son, John, with whom the portrait has traditionally been identified, was an attendant on Wolsey in 1521, and probably again in 1527, during his embassy to France. Later he seems to have resided on his estates in Cornwall, where in 1535 he was sheriff and connected with various county commissions till 1546. William, the younger son of John Reskimer the Elder, was the subject of a correspondence in the *Times Literary Supplement* in 1921, when the Rev. J. Kestell Floyer pointed out (15 September, p. 596; see also 22 and 29 September, and 13 October) that it was probably him, and not John the Younger, whom Holbein depicted. William was Page of the Chamber in 1532 and thereafter remained at Court, enjoying various small privileges and stewardships. In 1542 he received a grant of chambers within the Blackfriars, and became Gentleman Usher in 1546.

32. A GENTLEMAN : UNKNOWN (12258).

On a pale pink priming, $10\frac{13}{16} \times 8\frac{5}{16}$ in. (275 × 211 mm.): chalks: black, red (face); reinforced with washes of indian ink (hat, hair), and in indian ink with the pen (eyebrows, beard, etc.) and point of the brush (gown). Inscribed by the artist *atlass* (silk), *at* (lass), (twice) and *S* (? satin).

One of the best preserved and most impressive drawings of the series. The brushwork is of assured mastery and above all suspicion of being added. Hollar's etching of 1647 (Parthey 1547; *Klassiker der Kunst*, p. 199) renders the figure in reverse enclosed within a circle; see above, p. 12. It does not name the subject. Three identifications have been put forward, but none is supported by evidence. Lodge refers to Charles Brandon, Duke of Suffolk, and Edward Stafford, Duke of Buckingham, but without substantiating either belief. M. F. S. Hervey (*Holbein's 'Ambassadors,'* 1900. pp. 139-140), while admitting a discrepancy in dates, contends that the drawing is probably of Jean de Dinteville, the man standing on left in the National Gallery picture of 1533. But the resemblance is only a general one, and how fundamentally unlike the two portraits really are is emphasized by the completely convincing identification as Dinteville of a drawing by Clouet at Chantilly (*Burlington Magazine*, Vol. v (1904), p. 413). Ganz's suggestion that the unknown man may have been French seems rather plausible. He speaks of two reversed copies in New York and Oslo. For an interesting forgery (also reversed) based on the drawing, see M. J. Friedländer, *On Art and Connoisseurship,* 1942, plate 31.

33. A GENTLEMAN : UNKNOWN (12259).

On a pale pink priming, $11\frac{3}{4} \times 8\frac{3}{4}$ in. (298 × 222 mm.): chalks: black, red (face, detail of a ? chain near left upper corner), brown (hair), yellowish-brown (beard), white (? body-colour: traces in face, shirt); reinforced with the pen in indian ink (eyes, nose, moustaches). Eyes: grey-blue.

FIG. XV. HANS HOLBEIN : A GENTLEMAN, UNKNOWN (METROPOLITAN MUSEUM, NEW YORK)

Rather rubbed, but otherwise in fair condition. Ganz refers only to retouching in black chalk (which is correct); the penwork is of good quality and may be accepted as Holbein's. The page shows a number of small holes of the kind described above, p. 37.

The date is established as 1535 by the fact that the drawing corresponds with a small circular portrait on panel in the Metropolitan Museum, New York (Bache Collection; Fig. XV), which is inscribed ANNO DOMI 1535 . . . . ETATIS SVÆ 28. It shows the drawing to have been considerably cut on right. In the painting the man's nose has a pronounced, rather narrow ridge, but this high-light has almost completely vanished from the drawing. Ganz (*Jahrbuch für Kunst und Kunstpflege in der Schweiz*, 1921/24, p. 293-5) considers the costume to be that of a Frenchman, and even conjectures that the man might be one of the brothers of Jean de Dinteville. There is little or nothing to support either contention.

34. SIR NICHOLAS POYNTZ (12234).

On a pale pink priming, $11\frac{3}{16} \times 7\frac{3}{16}$ in. (284 × 183 mm.): chalks: black (stumped in collar), red (face), brown (hair), yellow (with red, chain, decoration on brim of hat); reinforced with the pen in indian ink (face, hair, etc.). Inscribed (gold and scarlet) near the upper corners **N Poines . . . Knight**. Left lower corner restored.

The chalks are rather badly rubbed. The penwork, though fairly skilful, is not of the best quality, and it is doubtful whether all of it can be by Holbein.

There are various pictures and miniatures corresponding with the drawing. Among the former, the finest is the property of the Earl of Harrowby, at Sandon Hall, on which see A. B. Chamberlain, Vol. II, p. 312. It is not, as stated by Chamberlain, identical with a version formerly in the possession of the Marquis de la Rosière (repr. *Klassiker der Kunst*, p. 217). These and other versions, at Althorp, Ince Blundell Hall, and in the possession of the Marquis of Bristol, are inscribed with a device in French, and give the date as 1535 and sitter's age as 25. Ganz refers to a miniature in the Ethel Hughes Collection, New York, at one time the property of Horace Walpole. This is not identical with the miniature in the Holford Sale, 13 July, 1927, lot 118, acquired by Sir Robert Abdy.

Sir Nicholas Poyntz, son of Sir Anthony Poyntz (?1480-1533), born 1510; died 1557. He married Joan, daughter of Thomas, Lord Berkeley. He is said (*D.N.B.*, Vol. XVI, p. 278) to have been a 'prominent courtier' during the latter part of Henry VIII's reign. Ganz's statement that he became Vice-Chamberlain to Queen Elizabeth is an obvious mistake, due to a confusion with his son-in-law, Sir Thomas Heneage.

35. SIMON GEORGE OF QUOCOUTE (12208).

On a pale pink priming, $11\frac{1}{16} \times 7\frac{5}{8}$ in. (281 × 193 mm.): chalks: black, red (face), yellow (moustaches, beard), white (? high-lights in face); extensively reinforced in indian ink with the brush (hat) and pen (hair, moustaches, etc.). Inscribed (gold and red) near the lower margin to right of centre **S. George of Cornwall.**

Well preserved and of fine quality, but retouched with metal-point along the lines indicating the garments. The relation of the drawing to the Frankfurt picture (Fig. VII; *Klassiker der Kunst*, p. 139, shows it before being restored to its original circular shape) is anomalous. They are certainly connected, but unlike every other such case, there are marked differences in the proportions, the shape of nose and ear, to say nothing of the beard, for which see above, p.22.

According to Lodge, Simon George was of Gloucestershire extraction, related to the Hussey family on his mother's side, and by marriage to the Lanyons of Cornwall, his wife being Thomasine, daughter of Richard Lanyon.

36. SIR CHARLES WINGFIELD (12249).

On a pink priming, $11\frac{1}{8} \times 7\frac{12}{16}$ in. (286 × 198 mm.): chalks: black, red (face, touches in beard, etc.), brown (beard), yellow (moustaches); reinforced with the pen in indian ink (beard). Inscribed (gold and scarlet) near the upper margin in centre **Charles Winhfield Knight.** Scarred across the right eyebrow.

Though omitted by Ganz, the drawing has every appearance of an original by Holbein. It seems, however, to have been somewhat retouched along the outline of the left shoulder and elsewhere. The penwork is not very good and may also be later.

An old and excellent copy (*Burlington Magazine*, Vol. XVIII (1910/11), p. 269; Vasari Society, 2nd Series, IX, plate 17) is in the Boymanns Museum, Rotterdam (from the Lanière, Sir John Leslie, and Koenigs Collections). It does not, however, show the full understanding of an original replica (which it has been claimed to be), as may be seen from the lines about the neck and chest. Wingfield is in fact represented in the Windsor drawing with the upper part of his body nude, and with an oval medallion suspended on his hairy chest by a ribbon forming a noose around his neck. Lodge suggests 'that the artist, having sketched a naked figure . . . . afterwards hinted the appearance of a light drapery.' This confusion is possibly due to some extent to an accidental smear or stain extending upwards beyond the shoulder line; but if that is so, the copyist was also so deceived, since he makes the subtly rendered ribbon of the original appear like the edge of a close-fitting garment. He omits the detail sketch, in the left upper corner, which, though not altogether clear, seems to represent a wrist encircled by a bracelet passed through a large finger-ring, the latter being set with a stone.

FIG. XVI. SIR CHARLES WINGFIELD. OLD COPY OF THE DRAWING NO. 36 AT
WINDSOR (BOYMANS MUSEUM, ROTTERDAM)

The sitter's identity is obscure. Lodge believed him
to be the son of Sir Richard Wingfield (?1469-1525),
soldier and diplomatist, on whom see *D.N.B.*, Vol. LXII,
p. 187. This Charles Wingfield, however, is not known to
have been knighted.

37. NICHOLAS BOURBON THE ELDER (12192).

On a (rather pale) pink priming, $12\frac{1}{8} \times 10\frac{1}{4}$ in. (309×260
mm.): chalks: black (partly stumped), red (touches in
face), brown (with black, in hair), white (collar); reinforced with the pen in indian ink (profile, eye, beard).
Inscribed (tarnished gold and crimson) in left upper
corner **Nicholas Borbonius Poeta**. There is a vertical
line on left, about $1\frac{3}{4}$ in. from the margin, as in Nos. 43
and 71.

The penwork, resembling that in Nos. 34 and 36, is rather doubtful.
The work in chalk is rubbed and in places perhaps retouched; left-
handed shading, however, remains plainly noticeable. No picture is
known, but the date is determined as 1535 by a woodcut after Holbein
(Fig. XVII; Woltmann, II, p. 185, No. 208), which was based on the
drawing and renders the figure in the reverse direction, but still using
his right hand to write. It is dated 1535, and first appeared in books
printed by Sebastian Gryphius at Lyons in 1536; see C. Dodgson in
Mitteilungen der Gesellschaft für vervielfältigende Kunst, 1908, p. 37.

Nicholas Bourbon or Borbonius, court preceptor and
poetaster, born at Troyes in 1503; died after 1550. He
repeatedly addressed verses to Holbein. His *Nugae*, a

collection of Latin poems, were praised by Joachim du
Bellay to the effect that *in toto libro nil melius titulo*. For
general accounts, see Nicéron, *Memoires pour servir à
l'histoire des hommes illustres*, Vol. XXVI (1734), p. 48, and
Michaud, Biographie Universelle (nouv. éd.), Vol. V, p. 286.
Neither of the above makes reference to the incident
which brought him to England in 1535 to pay homage
to Henry VIII and Anne Boleyn. It was in gratitude
for help received from them while under persecution in
France. The data relevant to this incident given by
Woltmann, Ganz and others, derive almost verbatim
from a particularly erudite note by Lodge.

VOL. XVII. NICHOLAS BOURBON. WOODCUT AFTER HOLBEIN

38. SIR RICHARD SOUTHWELL (12242).

On a pink priming, $14\frac{9}{16} \times 11\frac{1}{6}$ in. (370×281 mm.):
chalks: black, red (stumped in face, stripes in gown),
yellow (chain), light brown (eyebrows); reinforced in
indian ink with the pen (face) and brush (hat, hair); the
lines of the dress worked over incisively with metal
point. Inscribed by the artist in black chalk ANNO
ETTATIS SVÆ / 33 (the first and last letters partly cut
away) and annotated with the pen, vertically on right, *Die
augen ein wenig gelbatt* (the eyes a little yellowish). Inscribed (gold and scarlet) in left upper corner **Rich:
Southwell Knight**.   Immediately below ANNO is a
stain caused by the deletion of a cursive inscription of
which only the first two letters of the Christian name are
still plainly visible. There are three patched holes in the
face.

The condition is on the whole fairly good; but the sharp indentations
with metal-point are, as elsewhere, somewhat disturbing. It is possible
that these were neither in the nature of reinforcements nor of
retouchings, but connected with the transference of the design to the
panel. The interesting note on the colour of the eyes deserves notice.
It would seem that the eyes are actually rendered by a combination
of black, red and yellow chalks. The drawing is a study for the

FIG. XVIII. HANS HOLBEIN : SIR RICHARD SOUTHWELL (FLORENCE, UFFIZI)

picture of 1536 in the Uffizi in Florence (Fig. XVIII) which is inscribed x°IVLII ANNO/ H.VIII XXVIII°/ETATIS SVÆ/ANNO XXXIII. A copy is in the Louvre (*Klassiker der Kunst*, p. 218). The pictures include the right arm with the right hand resting on the left.

Richard Southwell, courtier and official, born 1504; agent of Cromwell in the dissolution of the monasteries, 1535-39; M.P. for Norfolk, 1539; knighted 1542; Master of the Ordnance, 1554-60; died 1563/4.

39. QUEEN JANE SEYMOUR (12267).

On a pale pink priming, $19\frac{13}{16} \times 11\frac{5}{16}$ in. (503×287 mm.): chalks: black, red (touches in face), yellow (folded lappet of headdress), brown (with yellow, forehead rolls of headdress); reinforced with the pen in indian ink (eyes, nose, mouth, contour of face) and with metal-point (outlines principally in lower part of drawing). Inscribed (gold and scarlet) in left upper corner **Iane Seymour Queen**. There is a horizontal join in the paper about $2\frac{1}{2}$ in. from the lower margin. Two other lines run horizontally across the drawing ($8\frac{1}{4}$ in. and $2\frac{2}{3}$ in. from bottom).

Like No. 13 this very famous drawing shows the characteristic "tiredness," due to incessant fingering, which only some of the less notable items of the series have really escaped. Retouching in black chalk is very noticeable in the necklace. The work in metal-point, as in No. 38, raises particular problems. The date is certainly 1536/37, and the artist seems to have used the study repeatedly. According to Ganz, it corresponds in size exactly with the Vienna picture (Fig. XIX) which, however, is in three-quarter length and differs in that the necklace (but not the pendant jewel attached to it) is of a more elaborate design. The same difference is noticeable

in a later version of the portrait at Woburn, reproduced by Fletcher and Walker, *Historical Portraits 1400-1600*, 1909, facing p. 124. The necklace of large pearls, as in the drawing, occurs in a copy or work-shop replica at The Hague (*Klassiker der Kunst*, p. 195), which also ends just below the hands. As a full-length figure, the Queen appeared in the same pose in the Whitehall mural painting, now destroyed.

Jane Seymour, third Queen of Henry VIII, daughter of Sir John Seymour, born (?) 1509; was lady-in-waiting to Queens Catherine and Anne; married 1536; died 1537, soon after the birth of Prince Edward.

FIG. XIX. HANS HOLBEIN : QUEEN JANE SEYMOUR (VIENNA MUSEUM)

40. LADY BOROUGH (?)

On a pale pink priming, $10\frac{3}{4} \times 7\frac{13}{16}$ in. (273×198 mm.): chalks: black, red (face), yellow (forehead rolls of headdress), brown (eyebrows). Inscribed (gold and scarlet) in left upper corner **The Lady Borow**.

The outline of the face on right, and of the eyes, has been lightly worked over. The whole is considerably rubbed. A picture is not known.

The identity of the sitter is obscure, and it may well be that the inscription is wrong. Lodge believed her to be Catherine (Clinton), wife of William, fourth Baron Burgh (Bourgh or Borough) of Gains-borough; but this seems incompatible with the fact that the latter was born as late as 1522, a date established by his age (twenty-eight) on his succession to the title in 1550. Ganz (quoting Hon. C. Stuart-Wortley) considers it a moot point whether the lady was the first or second wife of Thomas, third Baron Burgh. Neither alternative is in fact convincing. Agnes (Tyrwhitt), the first, was married (presumably in childhood) in 1496, a date conflicting with the age of the subject portrayed. On the other hand, Alice (London), the second wife, had been twice previously married before becoming Lady Burgh, and was not widowed for the first time till 1538. See Vicary Gibbs, *Complete Peerage*, Vol. II (1912), p. 423.

41. A LADY: (PRINCESS MARY?) (12220).

On a salmon pink priming, 15$\frac{3}{16}$ × 11$\frac{1}{2}$ in. (386 × 291 mm.): chalks : black, brown (traces in forehead rolls of headdress), yellow (pendant), red (lips, gable of headdress); reinforced with the pen in indian ink (outlines of face, etc.). Inscribed (gold and red) in left upper corner **The Lady Mary after Queen.** The left and lower margins are skirted at a distance of about $\frac{3}{4}$ in. by intersecting lines.

The drawing is obviously in a ruinous state, having been almost obliterated by rubbing and retouched by an insensitive hand. But there can be no doubt that it was originally by Holbein, although probably a slight and summary sketch. Left-handed shading is still perceptible in the fall of the headdress on left.

An etching by Hollar (Parthey 1465; *Klassiker der Kunst*, p. 199) renders the figure in reverse within a circle. It is inscribed *ex Collectione Arundeliana 1647* and named *Princeps Maria, Henrici Regis Angliae filia.* Recent opinion has been generally agreed that this identification is unfounded, though G. S. Davies (*Hans Holbein the Younger*, pp. 176-7) went as far in the opposite direction as to admit that it is not in the last instance irreconcilable with Mary's portrait in later years by Moro. A more appropriate comparison could be drawn with the Corvus portrait of 1544, showing Mary at the age of 28 (repr. Fletcher and Walker, *Historical Portraits 1400-1600*, 1909, plate facing p. 60), and a further word of caution should be spoken against a too hasty rejection of the drawing as a likeness of the future Queen. In 1536, when Mary was temporarily reconciled to her father, her age was twenty, which is approximately that of the girl portrayed, as far as can be seen from the drawing in its present condition. The magnificence of her jewellery, moreover, would speak for a personage of exalted station.

42. EDWARD, LORD CLINTON (12198).

On a pale pink priming, 8$\frac{13}{16}$ × 5$\frac{13}{16}$ in. (223 × 147 mm.): chalks: red (lips, corners of eyes, etc.), brown (over black in hair), yellow (moustaches, beard, plume); silver point (collar, under-garment); reinforced with the pen (?) in indian ink (line of mouth). Inscribed by the artist *?Silb* (for *Silber*, silver) or (?) *Silk*; *Dofat* (taffeta), *S* (? for *Sammet*, velvet). Inscribed (gold and scarlet) in left upper corner **Clinton.**

Some slight retouches are noticeable, for instance, about the ear, neck and hair, but generally the drawing is in good condition. A picture is not known. Date: about 1534/35.

Edward (Clinton, otherwise Fiennes), ninth Lord Clinton, born 1512; succeeded to title, 1517; attended Henry VIII at Boulogne and Calais, 1532; knighted 1534; Chief Captain of Boulogne, 1548-50; Lord High Admiral 1550-53, 1557/8-1584/5; Gentleman of the Privy Chamber, 1550; Knight of the Garter, 1551; Constable of the Tower, 1553; commanded expedition

at St. Quentin, 1557; Joint Commander against Northern Rebels, 1569; created Earl of Lincoln, 1572; died 1584/5.

43. SIR THOMAS STRANGE (12244).

On a pale pink priming, 9$\frac{5}{8}$ × 8$\frac{3}{8}$ in. (244 × 212 mm.): chalks: black (partly stumped), red (face, neck), yellow (moustaches), blue (iris of eye, a touch at collar on right), white (collar). Inscribed (gold and scarlet) near left upper corner **Tho: Strange Knight.** There is a small water-stain near the ear, and a faint vertical line on left as in Nos. 37 and 71.

The effect is very sensitive and delicately colourful, but some of the outlines (nose, collar, etc.) seem to have been lightly worked over. It is interesting to observe that the three roughly vertical lines joining the outline of the collar on left are in the picture (about to be described) narrow hanging strings or ribbons, of which others appear on right. The picture (*Klassiker der Kunst*, p. 109) was lent by Mr. Hamon le Strange to the Tudor Exhibition (1890), No. 113, and the Early English Portraiture Exhibition (B.F.A.C., 1909), No. 41. It bears a later or retouched inscription ANNO D^e 1536.... ÆTATIS SVÆ 43. To this picture, in which the sitter looks older, the drawing stands in a direct, but somewhat anomalous relation.

Sir Thomas Strange, or le Strange, son of Robert Strange of Hunstanton, born 1493; Esquire to the Body to Henry VIII; married Anne, sister of Thomas, Lord Vaux (No. 24); knighted and present at the Field of the Cloth of Gold, 1520; High Sheriff of Norfolk, 1532; Commissioner of Enquiry on revenues of Walsingham Abbey, 1536; died 1545.

44. A GENTLEMAN : UNKNOWN (12260).

On a pink priming, 10$\frac{13}{16}$ × 7$\frac{1}{2}$ in. (274 × 191 mm.): chalks: black, red (face), yellow (decoration on brim of hat), brown (eyes, beard); reinforced in indian ink with the pen (eyebrows, moustaches, beard, etc.) and brush (hat near plume and at outline of cheek-bone, hair to left of ear); heightened with white body-colour.

Described by Wornum as being 'in good condition,' this drawing is, in fact, somewhat problematical in regard to its present state of preservation. The rendering of the ear, and of the hair contiguous to it, is very weak. The beard, side-whiskers and moustaches are niggling, and the brushwork in the hat by no means convincing. There has probably been a good deal of retouching. A picture is not known.

45. A LADY : UNKNOWN (12255).

On a rather pale pink priming, 11$\frac{3}{8}$ × 9 in. (288 × 228 mm.): chalks: black (partly stumped), red (face), yellowish-brown (forehead rolls of headdress); reinforced with the pen in indian ink (eyebrows, lashes, pupils, nose, mouth). Eyes: grey-blue. Annotated by the artist *S Sam̄* (? for *schwarz Sammet*, black velvet), *Satin*, and *S Satin*, on right.

The lappets and fall of the headdress have possibly been strengthened, but the condition generally is fair, and the penwork good and sensitive. The drawing is worth considering as a possible companion to the preceding item. In the opinion of Ganz the connexion is between Nos. 44 and 49.

46. EDWARD, PRINCE OF WALES (12200).

On a pink priming, $10\frac{1}{2} \times 8\frac{7}{8}$ in. (267×226 mm.): chalks: black, red (face), yellow (hair on forehead); retouched with the pen in indian ink (eyes, nose, mouth). Inscribed (tarnished gold and crimson) near left upper corner **Edward Prince.**

No doubt always a very slight drawing, it has been badly rubbed and certainly reworked by a later hand. The outline of a puffed sleeve on left is evidently false. The head corresponds with the picture (Fig. XX) formerly in the Hannover Museum, now in the National Gallery at Washington, D.C. (Mellon Collection). Another good, but not original, version, formerly in the Yarborough Collection, is reproduced by A. B. Chamberlain, Vol. II, facing p. 166. It was engraved by Hollar, in 1650, when in the possession of Lord Arundel (Parthey 1395).

FIG. XX.   HANS HOLBEIN : EDWARD, PRINCE OF WALES (NATIONAL GALLERY OF WASHINGTON)

It is generally assumed that the Washington picture is identical with one presented by the artist to the King and listed in a roll of New Year's gifts for 30 Hen. VIII. This roll, first mentioned by Walpole, was shown to the Antiquarian Society in 1736, and is now in the Folger Shakespeare Library at Washington (Seymour de Ricci, *Census of MSS. in U.S.A.*, I, p. 296). Tempting as it might seem to conjecture that this roll referred actually to gifts received by the King on 1 January, 1540, not 1539, an assumption which would harmonize far better with the apparent age of the child in the Washington picture, the fact remains that it is specifically dated *First daie of January, anno XXX*, whereby the age of the child in the portrait referred to is established as little more than one year, according to the time taken to paint the picture. It is therefore somewhat doubtful whether the picture described in the roll can rightly be identified with that at Washington, in which, with all allowance for flattery to the Royal father, it seems impossible to assume that the age of the child was less than about two.

Edward, son of Henry VIII and Jane Seymour, born 12

October, 1537; ascended the throne 22 January, 1546/7; died 6 July, 1553.

47. A LADY : UNKNOWN (12190).

On a pale pink priming, $10\frac{11}{16} \times 6\frac{5}{8}$ in. (271×169 mm.): chalks: black, red (face), brown (eyes, hair); reinforced with the pen in indian ink (face, hair, collar, etc.); heightened with the brush in white body-colour (coif). Annotated by the artist in ink *Samat* (velvet) and *Damast* (damask); and by an XVIII century hand on the reverse *hans holbein*. The drawing has been cut along the contours of the headdress and shoulders, and imposed on a new sheet of primed paper (sizes as above). Collections: J. Richardson, Sen. (Lugt 2184); Richard Mead; Walter Chetwynd. Incorporated in the Royal Collection as the gift of Mr. Benjamin Way (see above, p. 21).

In spite of being very much rubbed, the drawing remains, thanks to the exquisite quality of the penwork, one of the most beautiful of the whole series. A picture is not known.

Even though at a comparatively recent date certain authorities such as Sir Richard Holmes have accepted the sitter's identity as Anne of Cleves, this is certainly wrong, and there is only the frontal pose in common between the drawing and the Queen's portrait of 1539 in the Louvre (*Klassiker der Kunst*, p. 124). Hollar's etching, Parthey 1343, is likewise unrelated. Wornum's conjecture (p. 413) that the subject might be Amelia, the sister of Anne of Cleves, though attractive and specious, and not like the other demonstrably wrong, remains nevertheless purely fanciful. All that is known is that such a portrait was carried out by Holbein when, in July, 1539, he travelled to Düren to paint the prospective Queen. See A. B. Chamberlain, II, p. 176.

48. A LADY : UNKNOWN (12256).

On a rose pink priming, $11\frac{3}{8} \times 8\frac{11}{16}$ in. (289×220 mm.): chalks: black (partly stumped), red (face), yellow (collar, coif on right), brown (hair). Annotated by the artist at lower margin in centre *damast sh. . . . .* (black damask).

It seems hardly possible that the lines of the spencer can be otherwise than reworked or transferred by indentation, lacking, as they do, all sensitiveness of touch. The face is considerably rubbed. A picture is not known. No evidence is available as to the sitter's identity, but W. Stein (*Holbein*, 1929, p. 303) may be right in saying that the lady was probably not English. Ganz confuses the drawing with the next (No. 49) when referring to Wornum's conjecture that it might be of Anne Boleyn.

49. A LADY : UNKNOWN (12254).

On a pale pink preparation, $11 \times 7\frac{11}{16}$ in. (279×195 mm.): chalks: black, red (face), yellow (hat-badge, hair, eyebrows); reinforced in indian ink with the pen (face) and brush (collar; more diluted, over yellow, in hair); touched with bluish body-colour (eyes).

The chalks are much rubbed, in fact the bust, arms and hands are hardly visible. Some of the ink lines are of fair quality, but the passages about the brow are not good. A picture is not known. Wornum's belief that the sitter might be Queen Anne Boleyn is certainly incorrect. Though not conclusive, Ganz's suggestion that the drawing might form a pair with No. 44 is worthy of consideration.

50. SIR PHILIP HOBY (12210).

On a pink priming, $11\frac{3}{4} \times 8\frac{15}{16}$ in. (298 × 226 mm.): chalks; black, red (face), brown (moustaches, beard). Eyes: bluish-grey. Inscribed (gold and reddish) below in centre **Phillip Hobbie Knight.** An impressed fingerprint occurs on the outline of the shoulder on left.

No doubt extensively stumped in the first place, the drawing has been further rubbed and softened. There are some obvious retouchings in black chalk, particularly the contour of the forehead and of the hat on left. Near the middle of the hat left-handed shading is discernible. A picture is not known.

Sir Philip Hoby, diplomatist, born 1505; Envoy to the Courts of Spain and Portugal, 1535-6; Gentleman Usher, 1541/2; knighted after the siege of Boulogne, 1544; Ambassador to Charles V, 1548; Privy Councillor and Master of Ordnance, 1552; Ambassador in Flanders, 1553; died 1558.

Holbein and Philip Hoby were on several occasions travelling companions in 1538 while jointly employed in the royal quest for a bride. Between 2 and 18 March they were at Brussels to obtain a portrait of the Duchess of Milan; in June they visited Le Havre for a similar purpose in regard to Louise de Guise, and possibly also Marie or Marguerite de Vendôme; two months later they betook themselves to Nancy and Joinville for sittings with Renée de Guise and Anne de Lorraine. See A. B. Chamberlain, Vol. II, Chaps. XX and XXI.

51. LADY HOBY (?) (12211).

On a pink priming, $10\frac{15}{16} \times 8$ in. (278 × 203 mm.). chalks: black, red (face), brown; reinforced in indian ink with pen (eyes, nose, mouth, chin) and brush (bonnet). Inscribed (gold and scarlet) in left upper corner **The Lady Hobbei.**

The drawing has suffered greatly from rubbing and has been much disfigured by later reinforcement in indian ink. Holbein's authorship may safely be assumed, though it has been too much obliterated to be readily visible. A picture is not known.

The sitter is identified by Lodge as Elizabeth (Cooke), wife of Sir Thomas Hoby, diplomatist and man-of-letters, younger half-brother of Sir Philip Hoby. But if the date of her birth is correctly recorded as 1528 (see D.N.B., Vol. IX, p. 950), this is manifestly impossible, unless the drawing is assumed to be by a later artist. In point of fact, there seems no reason to believe that the talented and interesting wife of the younger Hoby was the subject, rather than Elizabeth, daughter of Sir Walter Stoner, the wife of No. 50 of the present series.

52. EDWARD STANLEY, EARL OF DERBY (12243).

On a salmon pink priming, $11\frac{1}{8} \times 7\frac{13}{16}$ in. (283 × 198 mm.): chalks: black, red (lips, ear); reinforced in indian ink with the pen (eyes, moustaches, beard, etc.) and brush (outline of hat). Inscribed (gold and scarlet) in left upper corner **Edward Stanley Earle of Darbey.**

A large stain on the right side of the face has somewhat disfigured the drawing, which, in addition, must have been very much rubbed. The gown is now scarcely visible, while the hat has that blurred and porous appearance which one associates with offsetting. There has certainly been retouching in chalk about the collar. The penwork in the face is good, but unlike the ink line between the hat and forehead, the contour of the projection of the hat on left is rather feeble. A picture is not known.

Edward Stanley, third Earl of Derby (of the third creation), born 1509; succeeded 1521; Knight of the Bath and Cupbearer to Anne Boleyn, 1533; active in the suppression of the Northern Rebels, 1536-7; Knight of the Garter, 1546/7; Lord Lieutenant of Lancaster, 1552; Lord High Steward, 1553; Lord Lieutenant of Chester, 1569; died 1572.

53. GEORGE BROOKE, LORD COBHAM (12195).

On a pink priming, $11\frac{1}{2} \times 8\frac{1}{8}$ in. (291 × 206 mm.): chalks: black (stumped in hat and shadow of face), red (stumped, face and neck), yellow (chain, hat-badge), brown (eyes); touched with the pen in indian ink (? nostrils). Inscribed (tarnished gold and crimson) near left upper corner **Brooke Ld Cobham.**

The harder black chalk lines about the eyes, ears, neck, etc., are almost certainly retouchings of later date. But in general this splendid drawing is rather well preserved. A picture is not known. The date is presumably about 1538/40.

George Brooke, ninth Lord Cobham, born about 1497; knighted after capture of Morlaix, 1523; succeeded to the baronage, 1529; participated in trial of Anne Boleyn, 1536; Lieutenant General in Scottish campaigns, 1546, 1551; Knight of the Garter, 1549; implicated in Wyatt's rebellion, 1554, but pardoned; died 1558.

54. JOHN POYNTZ (12233).

On a pink priming, $11\frac{11}{16} \times 9\frac{1}{4}$ in. (297 × 235 mm.): chalks: black (partly stumped), red (face), brown (over black, hair), white (collar); reinforced with the pen in indian ink (face). Inscribed (dull gold and red) in left upper corner **Iohn Poines.**

The drawing shows a particular grandeur of conception, but has nevertheless been badly disfigured by later retouching. The penwork is coarse and scratchy, resembling that in No. 55. It is certainly not original. Left-handed shading is noticeable in the cap. A copy, formerly in the Heseltine Collection (repr. in *Original Drawings chiefly of the German School in the Collection of J.P.H.*, 1912, plate 21) is mentioned by A. B. Chamberlain (II, p. 71) as 'fine.' Actually it is extremely feeble. A version of the figure in oils, at Sandon Hall, to which Ganz refers, is interesting not only for giving the indication *Aet. Suae 42*, but for including a parapet along the bottom of the picture, and showing the contour of the sitter's back as the steeply falling curved line as in the drawing, but without the drapery drawn horizontally across it at the level of the shoulder.

John Poyntz, born about 1498, died 1558; was, according to Lodge, one of the lesser members of the Royal Household who attended Catherine of Aragon at the Field of the Cloth of Gold in 1520. He was of the younger branch of the Poyntz family; see Nos. 34 and 84.

55. ELIZABETH, LADY RICH (12271).

On a pink priming, $14\frac{15}{16} \times 11\frac{15}{16}$ in. (379 × 303 mm.): chalks: black, red (lips, eyelids), brown (forehead rolls of headdress, eyes); reinforced with the pen in indian ink (face) and with metal-point (outlines of dress, etc.). Annotated by the artist *Damast* (damask) and *Samet* (velvet) on the sleeve of the left arm. Inscribed (gold and scarlet) in left upper corner **The Lady Rich.**; below to left, at the level of the shoulder, ***The Lady Rich.***

The penwork is rather coarse and fumbling, and resembles that of No. 54. The drawing has also suffered greatly from rubbing. Left-handed shading is noticeable in the headdress on left. A picture, almost certainly a copy, corresponding with the figure, is in the Metropolitan Museum, New York (Fig. XXI; from the Croft Castle and Altman Collections). It extends the drawing considerably to the right, and includes the left arm and hand. See note to No. 80.

Elizabeth, daughter of William Jenks, or Gynkes, a London grocer, married Richard, first Baron Rich. Little more is recorded of her than that she died in 1558, having borne her scoundrel husband five sons and ten daughters.

FIG. XXI. COPY OF HANS HOLBEIN: LADY RICH (METROPOLITAN MUSEUM, NEW YORK)

56. KATHARINE, DUCHESS OF SUFFOLK (12194).

On a pale pink priming, $11\frac{7}{16} \times 8\frac{3}{8}$ in. (291 × 212 mm.): chalks: black, red (traces in face), yellow (forehead rolls of headdress, undergarment at bosom), brown (iris of eyes); reinforced in indian ink with the pen (eyebrows, lashes, nostril, line of mouth, gable of headdress) and brush (collar, etc.). Annotated by the artist *rot* (red, fillet of headdress) and *Damast* (damask, near lower edge in centre). Inscribed (gold and scarlet) near left upper corner **The Dutchefs of Suffolk.**

The drawing is rubbed and stained, and has a generally 'tired' appearance. The reinforced lines are of good quality. A picture is not

known. In the British Museum is a somewhat coarsened and damaged copy (omitting the notations in Holbein's hand), from the Lanière, Robinson and Malcolm Collections. See *Catalogue of Drawings by British Artists*, Vol. II, p. 329, No. 10; Ganz, plate C3.

The general character of the drawing would suggest a relatively early date in Holbein's second English period. Can the identification really be correct? Katharine, *suo jure* Baroness Willoughby de Eresby, daughter of William Willoughby de Eresby by his second wife, born 1518/9; granted in ward to Charles Brandon, Duke of Suffolk, and intended as the wife of his eldest son, Henry, Earl of Lincoln (died 1534); married the Duke of Suffolk as his fourth wife, 1534; became protestant 1539; widowed 1545; married Richard Bertie of Berested, about 1553; went into exile, 1554; returned after 1558; died 1580.

57. WILLIAM PARR, MARQUESS OF NORTHAMPTON (12231).

On a pink priming, $12\frac{1}{2} \times 8\frac{3}{8}$ in. (317 × 212 mm.): chalks: black (partly stumped), red (face), light brown (beard); reinforced with the pen and indian ink (extensively) and heightened with touches of white body-colour (eyes, end of nose). Annotated by the artist *wis felbet* (white velvet), *burpor felbet* (purple velvet), *wis satin* (white satin); and, among the details of ornament on left, *W* (for *weiss*, white, five times), *?Gl* (for gold, twice). The word *gros* appears in conjunction with a vertical line, indicating apparently a scale of measure; one of the details of jewellery is inscribed MORS. Inscribed (gold and discoloured red) to right of the head ***William Pa . . Marquis o(f) Northam(p): ton.***

The chalks are no doubt very much rubbed, but later retouching, if any, is negligible. The penwork is of excellent quality, and should be recognizable as Holbein's merely by comparison with such drawings as Ganz 100 or 150. There are no traces whatever of preliminary chalk lines under the penwork in the details of jewellery. The word MORS is presumably part of a motto, but did not occur in Northampton's personal device, which was *amour avecque loiaulté*. A picture is not known.

William Parr, brother of Queen Catherine Parr, born 1513; knighted about 1538; created Baron Parr, 1538/39; Knight of the Garter, 1543; created Earl of Essex, 1543; created Marquess of Northampton, 1546/7; Lord Great Chamberlain, 1549/50; attainted 1553; recreated Marquess of Northampton, 1558/9; died 1571.

58 ELIZABETH, LADY AUDLEY (?) (12191).

On a pale pink priming, $11\frac{5}{8} \times 8\frac{1}{4}$ in. (293 × 207 mm.): chalks: black, red (face, faint line in headdress), brown (hair), yellow (band in headdress); metal-point (jewellery); reinforced with the pen in indian ink (face). Annotated by the artist *samet* (velvet) and *rot damast* (red damask) in the dress; and on the brooch, *rot* (red), *w* (for *weiss*, white), (?) *Gl* (for gold), also the sign for green (a small heart-shaped leaf, as in No. 21). Inscribed (gold and scarlet) at the upper margin on left **The Lady . . . . Audley.** There is a stopped hole near the left shoulder.

The chalks are again badly rubbed, and there seems to be some re-working in the bonnet and right sleeve. The work is metal-point and pen is of the finest quality, and it is mainly to this that the drawing owes its beauty. Date: about 1540. A picture is not known, but a small circular miniature in the Royal Collection, Windsor Castle (Fig. XXII), corresponds closely in every detail.

FIG. XXII.   HANS HOLBEIN : MINIATURE OF LADY AUDLEY (WINDSOR CASTLE)

All is not clear about the sitter's identity, and in some respects the books are inaccurate. The lady may have been, as stated by Lodge, Elizabeth, daughter of Sir Brian Tuke and wife of George Tuchet, ninth Lord Audley. Chamberlain and Ganz speak of *John* Tuchet, ninth Lord Audley, which is certainly incorrect; John was, in fact, the eighth Baron, born 1483, died 1557; and though, to judge generally from age and date, it is unlikely that his wife, Mary Griffin, be represented, it would seem that there was a second Lady Audley of that time, Catherine, daughter of John Dackombe, of Stapleton. The date of the death of the ninth Baron's first wife is not definite; but it is possible that 'Elizabeth' Audley was in fact identical with Isabel Audley who died 1554, that is, three years before her husband succeeded to the title. But even if Elizabeth and Isabel are not identical, the former can only have ranked as Lady Audley for a very short time, since she must have died before January, 1559/60, when her husband is known to have contracted a second marriage. See Vicary Gibbs, *Complete Peerage*, Vol. I (1910), pp. 342-3.

59. AN ECCLESIASTIC : UNKNOWN (12199).

On a pink priming, $10\frac{9}{16} \times 8\frac{1}{16}$ in. (268 × 205 mm.): chalks: black, red (face), brown (traces in hair), white

(nose, cheek-bone); reinforced in indian ink with the pen (outline of nose, cheek) and brush (hair, chin, jaw, etc.); and with metal-point (lines of vestment). Inscribed (gold and red) at upper edge in centre **Iohn Colet Dean of St Paul's.**

Though the outlining of the cape is rather unconvincing, and the shading of the cap suggests a possible reinforcement of Holbein's left-handed hatchings, the work in ink is of the finest quality, and gives the face a particularly lively expression. The suggestion that the portrait was drawn, not from life, but from a picture of considerably earlier date, is therefore strangely misdirected (W. Stein, *Holbein*, 1929, p. 155).

That the inscription naming the sitter as John Colet (1467-1519) is manifestly wrong, was pointed out by Wornum and repeated by Woltmann. The identification, however, despite its obvious defiance of chronology, was accepted by Lodge; as early as 1620, moreover, an engraving by Arnold Buchel (Nagler, *Monogrammisten*, I, p. 76, No. 173), rendering the figure in the reverse direction and purporting to represent Colet, appeared in Holland's *Heroologia Anglica* (Vol. II, facing p. 145). From this engraving derives a very feeble picture in Magdalen College, Oxford (repr. Fletcher and Walker, *Historical Portraits*, 1909, I, plate facing p. 106). Neither a picture nor minia-ture directly connected with the drawing is known.

60. MARY, LADY MONTEAGLE (12223).

On a bright pink priming, $11\frac{3}{4} \times 7\frac{15}{16}$ in. (298 × 202 mm.): chalks: black, brown (hair), red (traces in face and brooch), yellow (touches in necklace); reinforced with the pen in indian ink. Annotated by the artist on the corsage *rot dammas* (red damask) and (in red chalk) *rot*; and on the headdress *rot*, *w* (for *weiss*, white) and ?*G.* . (? for gold). Inscribed (gold and scarlet) in left upper corner **The Lady Montegle.** The left lower corner is sloped and restored.

The drawing is badly rubbed. The penwork is surely original, though not as agreeable in effect as in the following drawing, which, how-ever, is similar in treatment and evidently of the same date. A picture is not known.

Ganz, following Lodge, considers it a moot question whether the subject was Mary Brandon, first wife of Thomas Stanley, second Lord Monteagle, or Ellen Preston, widow of Sir James Leybourne and second wife of Lord Monteagle. The occurrence of the jewelled letter M suspended from the lady's necklace does not provide useful evidence in either direction, since (like R in No. 16, and S in No. 19) it presumably refers to the title and not the Christian name. But in point of fact it seems certain from H. A. Doubleday and Lord Howard de Walden, *Complete Peerage*, Vol. IX (1936), p. 116, that only the first wife can be represented, since the date of the second marriage, though not precisely recorded, must be after 1544. Mary Brandon, born about 1510, died between 1540 and 1544.

61. A LADY : UNKNOWN (12253).

On a salmon pink priming, $11\frac{7}{16} \times 8\frac{1}{4}$ in. (290 × 210 mm.): chalks: black, red (face), brown (hair); reinforced in in-dian ink with the pen (face) and brush (dress, etc.). Annotated by the artist *rot* and *liecht rot damast* (light red damask) in the dress; *rot, w* (for *weiss*, white), *S* (? for schwarz, black), and (??) *Gold-ornament* in the headdress.

The omission by Chamberlaine and Holmes is unaccountable, but Ganz is mistaken in saying the drawing was not described by Woltmann and also that the reinforcing (which he considers to be later) is with the pen only. Far from being one of the most disfigured of the series, it is exceptionally well preserved and masterly in execution throughout. Date: about 1540. A picture is not known, and there is no clue to the sitter's identity.

62. A LADY : UNKNOWN (12218).

On a rather pale pink priming, $11 \times 7\frac{13}{16}$ in. (279×198 mm.): chalks: black (prominent only in headdress below on left), red (face, throat), brown (hair), yellow (band at crown of headdress); reinforced throughout with metal-point.

No doubt very much rubbed and considerably retouched; but it would be hard to believe that the work in metal-point was entirely alien. A picture is not known.

From Wornum's day to Ganz's, the idea has survived that the sitter might be Queen Catherine Howard. Though a certain resemblance may be admitted, it is nevertheless fairly conclusive that the features are not the same as in Catherine's portrait by Holbein in the J. H. Dunn Collection, or the miniatures at Windsor and in the Buccleuch Collection (*Klassiker der Kunst*, pp. 126, 148, 149).

63. A LADY : UNKNOWN (12189).

On a pale pink priming, $11 \times 7\frac{1}{2}$ in. (280×191 mm.): chalks: black, red (face), yellow (hair). Inscribed (gold and scarlet) in left upper corner **Anna Bollien Queen.**

Though this beautiful drawing is one of the few for which Ganz makes no specific mention of retouching, it has in fact probably been somewhat reinforced in black chalk by a later hand. A picture is not known. The inscription is certainly incorrect, the features showing no resemblance whatever with the well authenticated drawing of Anne Boleyn in Lord Bradford's possession (Ganz, 39). It is possible that there is indirect evidence of the sitter's identity in the occurrence of various heraldic sketches on the reverse of the drawing, these being of the coat-of-arms of the Wyatt family (Fig. XXIII).

The identification of the coat is due to Hon. Clare Stuart Wortley; see *Burlington Magazine*, Vol. LVI (1930), p. 211. The main sketch in centre shows an escutcheon with 1 and 4: per fesse azure and gules, a horse barnacle ringed argent; 2: gules, on a fesse or, between three boar's heads couped argent, three lions rampant sable; 3: argent on a bend gules, a martlet between two cinque foils or, a bordure engrailed azure bezantée. There are various notes of tinctures. On either side are subsidiary sketches: on right the escutcheon with a demi-lion as crest; on left a lion supporting the escutcheon. The suggestion may not be entirely fanciful that the identification of the obverse with Anne Boleyn was inspired by this coat-of-arms of Sir Thomas Wyatt, who was known to have been her lover before she became Queen. It is probable, but not certain, that the arms (which are not displayed on the lozenge proper to a female) are of the subject portrayed on the obverse side, and that she was therefore a lady of the Wyatt family. Two alternatives suggest themselves: Elizabeth (Brooke), wife of Sir Thomas Wyatt and daughter of George, Lord Cobham (No. 53); and Mary Wyatt, sister of Sir Thomas, a friend and lady-in-waiting of Anne Boleyn.

64. SIR THOMAS WYATT (12250).

On a pale pink priming, $14\frac{11}{16} \times 10\frac{11}{16}$ in. (373×272 mm.): chalks: black, red (face, patch at shoulder on left, another on chest), brown (beard); reinforced with the

FIG. XXIII. HANS HOLBEIN : HERALDIC SKETCHES ON REVERSE OF NO. 63

pen in indian ink (hair, beard). Eyes: grey-blue. Inscribed (gold and scarlet) in left upper corner **Tho: Wiatt
Knight**. The face is considerably stained.

The penwork is greatly superior to that in No. 65 and is certainly
by Holbein himself. The chalks are much rubbed, and the contour
of the hat is probably reworked. Date: about 1537 or later. A picture
is not known. Another portrait of Wyatt by Holbein is also lost. From
it derive the small circular woodcut (repr. Woltmann, I, p. 364),
which appeared in Leland's *Naeniae in mortem Thomae Viati*, 1542, and
two circular paintings, in reverse to the woodcut, in the Bodleian
Library and Natoinal Portrait Gallery.

Thomas Wyatt the Elder, poet and diplomatist, born (?)
1503; Clerk of the King's Jewels, 1524; Marshal of
Calais, 1529; Privy Councillor, 1533; imprisoned, 1536;
knighted 1537; Ambassador to Charles V, 1537-9; missions to Flanders and Paris, 1539/40; imprisoned 1540-41;
Knight of the Shire for Kent, 1542; died 1542; posthumous publication of poems in Tottel's *Miscellany*, 1557.

65. SIR THOMAS WYATT (12251).

On a rose pink priming, 14 $\frac{9}{16}$ × 10 $\frac{15}{16}$ in. (370 × 277 mm.):
same technique as No. 64. Inscribed (tarnished gold and
crimson) at upper margin to right of centre **Sr Tho: Wiat
K^t**

This is an old, close and very skilful copy of the preceding, the only
case in the Windsor series of an original and copy having been preserved together. The copyist was clearly a draughtsman of unusual
ability, and it might be permissible to hazard the guess that he was
Federico Zuccaro, who is known to have made copies of designs by
Holbein. The difference in quality between the two drawings is
nevertheless marked, the superiority of No. 64 being manifest at
first sight.

66. WILLIAM FITZWILLIAM, EARL OF
SOUTHAMPTON (12206).

On a pink priming, 15 $\frac{5}{16}$ × 10 $\frac{13}{16}$ in. (388 × 274 mm.):
chalks: black, red (face), brown (hair). The principal
outlines have been worked over with a sharp metal-
point. Inscribed (tarnished gold and crimson) **Fitz
Williams Earl of Southampton.**

Though omitted by Ganz, the drawing is of unimpeachable authenticity, indeed one of the most impressive and purest of the series. Left-
handed shading is plainly noticeable in the hat. The retracing of the
outlines with metal-point seems to have been done in the process of
transferring the design to the panel. Holbein's original picture is said
to have been destroyed by fire at Cowdray House in 1793, but a
copy, dated 1542, is in the FitzWilliam Museum, Cambridge (Fig.
XXIV), and shows a full length figure of particularly fine conception.
A further copy (misnamed Thomas More) of the head and shoulders
only belongs to the Duke of Devonshire (B.F.A.C.: *Exhibition of Early
English Portraiture*, 1909, No. 34, plate V). The contention (*ibidem*, p.
86) that the Cambridge picture is an original of Guillim Stretes (?),
the Master of the *Young Man in Red*, at Hampton Court, cannot be
upheld, though the evidence for the destruction of Holbein's original
is not forthcoming.

William FitzWilliam, born (?) 1490; knighted 1513;
Comptroller of the Royal Household and Knight of the
Garter, 1526; Lord Privy Seal, 1533; Lord High Ad-
miral, 1536-40; Earl of Southampton, 1537; died 1542.

FIG. XXIV.   COPY OF HANS HOLBEIN: WILLIAM, EARL OF SOUTHAMPTON
(FITZWILLIAM MUSEUM, CAMBRIDGE)

67. MARGARET, LADY BUTTS (12264).

On a pink priming, 15 × 10 $\frac{3}{4}$ in. (380 × 273 mm.): chalks:
black, red (face, throat), brown (forehead rolls of headdress); metal-point (fur collar, corsage); reinforced in
indian ink with the pen (face) and brush (collar). Inscribed (gold and scarlet) near left upper corner **The
Lady Buts.**

The condition of the drawing is rather problematical, but it seems
certain that there is a considerable amount of later retouching. Left-
handed shading is clearly visible in the headdress, and the reinforcing
of the collar is of good quality. Many of the other lines, however,
appear coarse and mechanical, and the upper contour of the forehead roll on left is very faulty. The study served for a picture in the
Gardner Museum, Boston (Fig. XXV; *Klassiker der Kunst*, p. 133),
inscribed ANNO ÆTATIS SVE LVII; the companion picture, representing
Sir William Butts, has an inscription ANNO ATATS SVE LIX. In neither
case is the date of birth exactly recorded; for Sir William it is pre-
sumed to be about 1485. The drawing is certainly of the end of
Holbein's activity.

FIG. XXV. HANS HOLBEIN : LADY BUTTS (BOSTON, GARDNER MUSEUM)

Margaret, wife of Sir William Butts, was the daughter of John Bacon, of the county of Cambridgeshire. She served as a lady-in-waiting to Princess Mary and married the King's physician, who also attended the Princess. She was living at the time of her husband's death in November, 1545.

68. A MAN : UNKNOWN (12221).

On a salmon pink priming, 11⅜ × 9¼ in. (288 × 235 mm.): chalks: black, red (face), light brown (hair); touched with the pen in indian ink (eyes, nostril, chin, ear). Inscribed (gold and scarlet) in left upper corner, **Phil: Melanchton.** There is a hole near the centre of the hat.

The drawing is deplorably rubbed and has been retouched at a later date with chalk as well as in ink. The penwork resembles that of No. 46. Left-handed shading is, however, still noticeable in the hat, which is enough to dispose of A. B. Chamberlain's suspicion (II, p. 250) that the draughtsman might be someone other than Holbein.

There is no resemblance with Holbein's authenticated portrait of Melanchton (*Klassiker der Kunst*, p. 92), nor with Cranach's, and Wornum was certainly right in assuming the drawing to be misnamed. Can Walpole have been of the same opinion? Among Vertue's copies listed in the description of Strawberry Hill the name of Nicholas Kratzer is found to occur, a fact which is hard to explain unless possibly the present portrait was thought by Walpole, again in error, to be the astronomer. The subject was evidently not a member of the nobility or courtier class, and it is not impossible that he was mistaken for Kratzer, though actually the Louvre portrait (*Klassiker der Kunst*, p. 73) shows a man of an altogether different appearance.

69. JOHN RUSSELL, EARL OF BEDFORD (12239).

On a pink priming, 13¾ × 11 9/16 in. (349 × 294 mm.):
chalks: black (partly stumped), red (face), brown (moustaches, upper part of beard), white (hair, beard). Eyes: grey-blue. Inscribed (gold and scarlet) along the upper margin **I Russell Ld Privy Seale . . . . with one Eye.**

The condition is rather good, but there seem to be some slight retouchings in black chalk for instance, the outline of the brow and skull-cap. The original picture for which the drawing served is lost, but a copy is at Woburn Abbey (repr. A. M. Tavistock and E. M. S. Russell, *Biographical Catalogue of the Pictures at Woburn Abbey*, 1890, Vol. I, plate facing p. 216). This shows the sitter wearing the collar of the Garter, with which he was invested in 1539. Being schematically painted, it might be questioned whether the collar appeared in the original version, but in any case the date could not be before 1539, and quite possibly indeed later. The disconcerting statement in J. E. Doyle's *Official Baronage* (1886, Vol. I, p. 154) that Russell lost the sight of his right eye in the campaign of 1544 against France is wrong. In fact, this occurred as early as 1522, as the result of an arrow wound at the assault of Morlaix; see *D.N.B.*, Vol. XLIX, p. 444.

John Russell, third Earl of Bedford (first of the second creation), born about 1485; Gentleman of the Privy Chamber, 1507; knighted 1522; created Baron Russell, 1538/9; Lord High Admiral, 1540-2; Privy Seal, 1542-55; created Earl of Bedford, 1549/50; Lord Privy Seal, 1553; died 1554/5.

70. LORD FRANCIS RUSSELL (12240).

On a rather bright pink priming, 9½ × 7⅛ in. (242 × 181 mm.): chalks: black, red (traces in face), brown (hair); retouched with the pen in indian ink (hair, eyes, nose, mouth, ear). Annotated by the artist *rot Damast* (red damask) on the coat. Inscribed (gold and scarlet) along the upper margin, **Francis Russel E: of Bedford *some time After.***

Very much rubbed and disfigured. The penwork is certainly not original. A picture is not known. Date: about 1540-42.

Francis Russell, fourth Earl of Bedford (second of the second creation), born 1527; Knight of the Bath, 1546/7; imprisoned 1553-55; succeeded his father, John Russell, as Earl of Bedford, 1555; escaped to the Continent and returned, 1558; Knight of the Garter, 1564; Lieutenant of the Garter, 1576; died 1585.

71. EDWARD, PRINCE OF WALES (?) (12201).

On a pale pink priming, 10 13/16 × 9 in. (275 × 229 mm.): chalks: black, red (face), pale yellowish (hair); reinforced with the pen in indian ink (contour of face, eyes, nose, mouth). Eyes: bluish-grey. Inscribed (tarnished gold and crimson) in left upper corner **Edward Prince of Wales.** A vertical line, as in Nos. 37 and 43, is visible on left. A long tear cuts diagonally across the left upper corner, touching the hair.

The present appearance of the drawing has been effected not a little both by retouching and rubbing. The penwork is surely not Holbein's. The rendering of the hair, too, is rather feeble. Traces of left-handed shading are noticeable in the hat and coat.

If the sitter is correctly named, the drawing can be reliably dated at 1542/43, when the Prince was five or six years of age. It might be, however, that the doubt which crossed Wornum's mind is not un-justified, and that his alternative suggestion that the boy was Henry Brandon, Duke of Suffolk (1535-1551), the elder of the two sons of Charles, Duke of Suffolk, by his last wife, Katharine Willoughby (No. 56), should be considered. There is undoubtedly some resem-blance with the Windsor miniature of Henry Brandon by Holbein; see *Klassiker der Kunst*, p. 149. But it should be remembered that Sir John Cheke acted as tutor both to Edward and Henry, and that, presuming the identification of the subject to conform with his, a confusion between the two would be doubly improbable. Ganz refers to derivative pictures (copies after Holbein) in Christ's Hospital, London, and a Scottish collection.

72. MARY ZOUCH (?) (12252)

On a pale pink priming, $11\frac{11}{16} \times 8\frac{3}{8}$ in. (296 × 212 mm.): chalks: black, red (face, touches in hair), yellow (neck-lace, ornamentation of headdress, with brown in hair), salmon pink (fillet in headdress), white (outline of *décol-letage*); reinforced with the pen in indian ink (eyes, nostrils, mouth). Annotated by the artist *black felbet* on bodice. Inscribed (gold and scarlet) in left upper corner **M Souch.**

One of the most beautiful of the series, the drawing has probably been somewhat retouched in black chalk along the outline of the boddice and elsewhere; but there seems no reason to impugn either the penwork or the flower, the latter appearing below in centre as if held in the hand, as in the pictures of Lady Vaux. Regarding the annotation in English, see above, note to No. 11. A picture is not known.

Mary Zouch, with whom the sitter is identified by A. B. Chamberlain (II, p. 259) and Ganz, was a maid-of-honour to Queen Jane Seymour, and the recipient in 1542 of an annuity for her services. But it is quite uncer-tain whether the first letter, M, of the inscription was intended as the initial of a Christian name (as in Nos. 34, 35, 69, 84) or as an abbreviation for *Mistress* (as S for *Sir* in No. 76). Lodge, followed by Wornum and Holmes, believed the lady to be Joan (Rogers), wife of Richard Zouch (died 1552), son and heir to John, Lord Zouch of Haringworth.

73. GRACE, LADY PARKER (?) (12230).

On a pink priming, $11\frac{1}{2} \times 8\frac{5}{16}$ in. (292 × 210 mm.): chalks: black, red (face), light brown (hair), yellow (nar-row band in headdress), pale orange-red (broad band in headdress). Inscribed (tarnished gold and crimson) near left upper corner **The Lady Parker.**

Rather rubbed, and perhaps somewhat retouched, but on the whole not much disfigured. A picture is not known.

The subject cannot be definitely determined, and has already given rise to some confusion. It is certain that the lady was neither Alice (St. John), wife of Henry Parker, Baron Morley (1476-1556), nor Jane (Parker), Lady Rochford, daughter of the above, who married in 1526 and played a sinister part in the tragedies of Anne Boleyn and Catherine Howard. (See G. S. Davies, *Hans Holbein the Younger*, 1903, p. 182.) It is safe to assume that in fact she was the first or second wife of Sir Henry Parker (son and heir presumptive of Henry, Lord Morley) who, dying in 1553, predeceased his father. The first wife, Grace (Newport), Lady Parker, married in 1523, aged 8; the second, Elizabeth Calthorpe, married in or before 1549, and was therefore not Lady Parker during Holbein's lifetime. The drawing

however, could have been made while she was still a spinster, and inscribed with the name of her first husband. But it is not very prob-able. From 1552 to after 1563 she was Lady Woodhouse; at the time of her death, in 1578, she was the wife of Dru Drury of Norwich.

74. A GENTLEMAN : UNKNOWN (12262).

On a pale pink priming, $10\frac{1}{4} \times 8$ in. (261 × 203 mm.): chalks: black, red (lips, corners of eyes, touches in beard), brown (hair), yellowish-brown (beard). Eyes: grey.

Though rubbed and softened in appearance, this drawing, omitted by Ganz, is skilful and lively, and links on readily with the next. There are probably retouchings at the shoulders, at the sides of the hat, and elsewhere. A picture is not known.

75. SIR WILLIAM SHARINGTON (12241).

On a salmon-pink priming, $11\frac{15}{16} \times 8\frac{1}{8}$ in. (304 × 206 mm.): chalks: black, red (lips, extremity of beard), brown (beard, with black in hair). Inscribed (gold and red) below in centre ***William Sharinton***, below which appears what resembles a *V*, but is doubtless a mutilated *K* in *Knight*. There are three unstopped holes; others near the right shoulder have been restored.

Much rubbed; the ear, contour of the forehead, etc., have clearly been retouched. A late drawing for which a picture is not known. Left-handed shading is visible in the hat.

Sir William Sharington, or Sherington, born about 1495; Page of the King's Robes; Vice-Treasurer of the Mint at Bristol, 1546; Knight of the Bath, 1546/47; perpetrated extensive frauds and joined the plots of Thomas Sey-mour; arrested 1548/49, but received pardon; Sheriff of Wiltshire, 1552; died 1553.

76. SIR GEORGE CAREW (12197).

On a salmon-pink priming, $12\frac{9}{16} \times 9\frac{1}{4}$ in. (319 × 235 mm.): chalks: black (partly stumped), red (face), brown (with black, moustaches, upper part of beard); sharply worked over with metal-point along the principal outlines. In-scribed (tarnished gold and crimson) in right upper corner **S. G. Carow Knight**, There is a black stain where on right the outline of the hat joins the face; also a smeared stain below in centre, similar to those (No. 18, etc.) where italic inscriptions have been partly deleted.

Ganz is uncertain whether this is an original drawing, much re-worked, or a copy after Holbein. The former is more probable; but that much injury has been caused by rubbing and reworking is evident. The drawing was used for a circular picture of fine quality, in the possession of the Earl of Bradford. It must date from the very end of Holbein's activity. It has an inscription SIR GEORGE CAREW/ KNIGHT FIRST SOHN TO SIR/WILLM CAREW DROWNED AT/PORTSMOUTH IN THE MARYROS.

Sir George Carew, soldier and naval commander, eldest son of William, Baron Carew of Mohuns Ottery, born (?) 1514; Captain of the tower of Ruysbanc, near Calais, 1540; Lieutenant-General of the Horse under Sir John Wallop, 1543/44; taken prisoner at Landrecy, 1544, but restored to liberty; Vice-Admiral to Dudley, Viscount Lisle, and in command of the *Mary Rose*, in 1545, at the time she foundered with all hands when leaving Portsmouth harbour to engage the French fleet.

77. SIR GAVIN CAREW (12196)

On a salmon pink priming, $10\frac{7}{8} \times 8\frac{9}{16}$ in. (275 × 216 mm.): chalks: black, red (lips, touches at eyes), brown (point of beard); reinforced with the pen in indian ink (collar, outlines of neck and hat on right) and sharply worked over with metal-point (all leading outlines). Inscribed (gold and scarlet) in the upper corners **Gawin Carow . . . Knight.** Water-stains in various places.

Very much injured and extensively reworked. Lodge refers to a picture of this subject in the possession of Lord de Clifford, at Kings Weston, near Bristol. Ganz mentions a miniature exhibited at Rotterdam in 1910.

Gavin, fourth son of Sir Edmund Carew and uncle to Sir George Carew (No. 76) and Sir Peter, his more famous brother; born 15..; married Anne Brandon, sister of the Duke of Suffolk and, secondly, Mary, Lady, Guildford, widow of No. 10; witnessed the sinking of the *Mary Rose*, 1545; Sheriff of Cornwall, 1547; involved in the Devonshire insurrection, 1553; attainted, imprisoned at Exeter, but escaped and pardoned; died 1583.

78. SIR JOHN GAGE (12207).

On a salmon pink priming, $15\frac{11}{16} \times 11\frac{1}{2}$ in. (398 × 291 mm.): chalks: black, red (face), brown (beard); reinforced in indian ink with the pen (beard) and brush (hair, hat, etc.), and, incisively, with metal-point (gown). Inscribed (gold and red) near left upper corner **Gage.**

The work in indian ink is devoid of skill or sensitiveness, and is certainly not by Holbein. But traces of left-handed shading appear in the hat, and there can be little doubt that the drawing, in spite of its injuries, is fundamentally an original of the master. A picture is not known.

The subject, according to Lodge, is Sir John Gage, statesman and military commander, born 1479; Comptroller of Calais, 1522; Vice-Chamberlain to the King, 1528-40; Knight of the Garter, 1532; Constable of the Tower and Comptroller of the Household, 1540; commanded the expedition against Scotland, 1542; besieged Boulogne, 1544; Lord Chamberlain, 1553; died 1556/57.

79. THOMAS, BARON WENTWORTH (12248).

On a salmon pink priming, $12\frac{1}{2} \times 11\frac{1}{8}$ in. (318 × 282 mm.): chalks: black, red (traces in face), brown (hair); reinforced in indian ink with the pen (eyes, nose, moustaches) and brush (hat near right eye); incised with metal-point for transfer (?). Inscribed (tarnished gold and red) in left upper corner **Ld Wentworth.**

Very much damaged and reworked, and lacking such evidence as left-handed shading to support the belief that Holbein was the draughtsman. A portrait of Lord Wentworth with the date 1547, by Hans Eworth, is at Wentworth Castle (*Walpole Society*, II (1912-13), p. 18, plate XIII), and seems to show the subject at a somewhat younger age.

Thomas Wentworth, first Baron Wentworth of Nettlestead, born 1501; knighted for bravery in France, 1523; raised to the Peerage, 1529; supported the royal divorce, 1530; attended the King to Boulogne, 1532; Privy Councillor, 1549-51; Lord Chamberlain, 1550; died 1551. He was a collateral ancestor of Anne Isabella (Millbanke), Lady Byron.

80. RICHARD, BARON RICH (12238).

On a pink priming, $12\frac{11}{16} \times 10\frac{7}{16}$ in. (322 × 265 mm.): chalks: black, red (? traces in face); reinforced with the pen in indian ink (outline of face, eyebrows, eyes, nose, mouth). Inscribed (gold, partly flaked, and scarlet) in left upper corner, **Rich Ld Chancelor.** A water stain crosses the whole of the lower part of the drawing horizontally; another stain near the left eye.

The drawing is perhaps the most ruined and obliterated of the series. There are traces, however, of left-handed shading in the hat which seem to suggest that it was fundamentally by Holbein. It may in that case have been the companion to No. 55.

Sir Richard Rich, first Baron Rich, born probably 1496; Solicitor-General, 1533; basely involved in the trials of More and Fisher; Knight of the Shire for Essex, 1536; raised to the Peerage, 1547/48; Lord Chancellor, 1548; resigned the Great Seal, 1551; founded Felstead Grammar School, 1564; died 1567.

81. SIR THOMAS PARRY (12232).

On a salmon pink priming, $10 \times 7\frac{6}{16}$ in. (254 × 186 mm.): chalks: black, red (face; some touches, appearing orange, at throat); touched with (?) the pen in indian ink (eyes, nostril, mouth). Inscribed (gold and scarlet) near left upper corner, **Thomas Parrie.** A hole near the left shoulder, unskilfully stopped.

Well preserved on the whole, though perhaps a little retouched about the hat and elsewhere. The attribution is particularly difficult. Ganz's omission of the drawing may not be unjustified; but in spite of a rather soft and flabby delineation, there is yet much of Holbein in it, and the way in which the hat badge is rendered in a separate sketch could not accord better with his common practice.

Thomas ap Harry, or Parrie, son of Henry Vaughan of Tretower and a distant kinsman of Sir William Cecil; probably an agent of Thomas Cromwell, about 1536-39; attended Princess Elizabeth during the reign of Queen Mary; knighted 1558; Privy Councillor and Comptroller of the Household, 1558; Master of the Court of Wards and Liveries, 1559; died 1560.

82. A GENTLEMAN : UNKNOWN (12261).

On a salmon pink priming, $13\frac{6}{16} \times 9\frac{7}{16}$ in. (338 × 239 mm.): chalks: black, red (lips), brown (eyes); reinforced (face) and washed (hat) with the brush in indian ink.

There is perhaps a trace of left-handed shading near the collar on left, but the drawing in its present state is much too coarsely and extensively worked over to admit of an even tentative opinion as to its original appearance. Apart from its injury due to reworking, it is disfigured by stains, badly touched over, in the right cheek.

In an article in the *Burlington Magazine* (Vol. LII (1928), pp. 278-283), a portrait of a man in the Uffizi was claimed to represent Sir Philip Hoby (above, No. 50), and the present drawing, but less positively, his brother, Sir Thomas Hoby, for which a verbal tradition is alleged to exist. Neither identification is at all convincing.

83. HENRY HOWARD, EARL OF SURREY (12213).

On a pink priming, 7½ × 8⅝ in. (191 × 144 mm.): metal-point; chalks: black (traces in outline of hat), red (face), brown (beard). Inscribed (gold and scarlet) along the upper margin. **Tho Howard . . . E: of Surrey.**

The drawing, though not without quality, differs manifestly in style from Holbein, and is certainly not by him. It might be by the same hand as a profile head of Henry Howard (correctly named in the inscription), which is in the Morgan Library, New York (repr. Fairfax Murray Collection, I, plate 259). Ganz (*Kritischer Katalog*, p. 19) refers to the present drawing as an inexact copy of a portrait by Holbein painted in 1542, of which there is an etching by Hollar (Parthey 1509; repr. *Klassiker der Kunst*, p.197), and which appears in the background of Philip Fruytiers' painting (after Van Dyck) showing Thomas and Aletheia, Earl and Countess of Arundel, with their grandchildren (in the possession of Lord Stafford; reproduced by M. F. S. Hervey, *Life of Thomas Howard*, 1921, pl. xxi). An interesting version of this portrait of Henry Howard, attributed to Holbein, was in the Berkeley Sheffield Sale, Christie's, 16 July, 1943, lot 52. This picture (inscribed *anno etatis suae 25*) and the present drawing differ in the direction of the head and eyes, and it is impossible that the latter should be even a free copy of the former. In *Klassiker der Kunst* (p. 250) Ganz speaks of it as a study for the picture.

84. A GENTLEMAN : UNKNOWN (12235).

On a rather bright pink priming, 11⅞ × 8¼ in. (301 × 210 mm.): chalks: black, red (face; touches of an orange tint in neck, ear, moustaches, beard). Inscribed (gold and scarlet) in left upper corner **N Poines Knight** and at the lower margin in centre **N Poines Knight** (partly deleted).

There is doubtless some later retouching, particularly in the hair. A picture is not known. The style differs not a little from Holbein's, and seems to partake of characteristics specifically French.

The inscription is evidently mistaken. The sitter seems to have been thought the same as No. 34, but this opinion is certainly wrong. Nor is Lodge's assumption, followed by Woltmann, correct, that we have here father and son of the same name. The relative ages and dates admit of no such conjecture; Lodge, moreover, identifies the older man (No. 84) with Nicholas, son of Sir Anthony Poyntz, who is in fact represented in the other drawing.

85. EDWARD, PRINCE OF WALES (12202).

On a pink priming, 10⅝ × 7 9/16 in. (276 × 192 mm.): chalks: black, red (face), yellow (hair, eyebrows). In-scribed (tarnished gold and crimson) in left upper corner **Edward VI.**

This feeble drawing has evidently been retouched, and something of its grotesque appearance is due to this, particularly to the misplaced pupil of the eye. Holbein's authorship is manifestly impossible; apart from all else, observe the consistently right-handed shading. W. Stein (*Holbein*, 1929, p. 310) connects the drawing with the profile of Henry Howard in the Morgan Library (see above, p. 17), and, but again unconvincingly, with the circular portrait of Prince Edward, aged 6, from the Lee of Fareham and Bache Collections, now in the Metropolitan Museum, New York. This picture, though not universally accepted, is obviously of a quality very greatly superior to the present drawing, and, while the nose is the same, differs from it in expression and details of costume and headdress.

(86). The male portrait listed by Wornum, p.407, No. 43, and there described as a copy (with a note connecting it with one of two items eliminated from the series 'of late years' as works of Jacob Binck) is almost certainly identical with Vertue's No. 189, and No. 47 of L. van Puyvelde's *Flemish Drawings at Windsor Castle*, 1942, p. 14 (12955). Its measurements are there given as 8 × 6 in., as compared with Vertue's 8⅛ × 6¼ in. The page is drawn on both sides (in black chalk on a pink priming), the subject in each case being the head of a man, three-quarters to right. The obverse side has a long inscription in Flemish. Puyvelde's attribution is to Cornelis van Cleef (1520-1567); see below, note to No. (87).

(87). The female portrait listed by Wornum, p. 413, No. 42, and connected by him, as in the preceding case, with one or two drawings eliminated from the series as works of Jacob Binck, seems to be identical with Vertue's No. 190 and L. van Puyvelde's No. 46 (12956). Its measurements are given by the latter as 8⅝ × 6¼ in. as compared with Vertue's 8½ × 6½ in. It represents a half-length figure of a woman wearing a coif, directed three-quarters to left, and is drawn in black and red chalks on a pink priming. Puyvelde's contention that this drawing is a preparatory study from the life for the Windsor picture reputed to be the wife of Joos van Cleef, is very unconvincing. There are marked differences of age and feature, costume and headdress, and only the general pose bears a superficial resemblance. See C. H. Collins Baker, *Catalogue of the Principal Pictures at Windsor Castle*, 1937, p. 56, plate 18. Whether the attribution to Cornelius van Cleef will prove acceptable is equally doubtful. Neither of the drawings, in any case, has any connexion, direct or indirect, with Holbein, and their elimination from this series was abundantly justified.

TABLE OF REFERENCES
AND INDEX OF NAMES

TABLE OF REFERENCES

LIST OF BIBLIOGRAPHICAL ABBREVIATIONS

[ARUNDEL]. *The Windsor Collection of Holbein Portraits of the Court of Henry VIII.* Five parts (80 plates). Published by the Arundel Society, 1877.

[BRAUN]. *Johann Holbein: le Livre de Portraits à Windsor Castle.* Choix de cinquante Dessins. 3rd ed., 1932.

[CHAMBERLAINE]. *Imitations of Original Drawings by Hans Holbein, in the Collection of His Majesty, for the Portraits of Illustrious Persons of the Court of Henry VIII.* Published by John Chamberlaine. Fol. 1792-1800. Quoted below from the 4to edition of 1812.

[GANZ]. (I) *Die Handzeichnungen Hans Holbeins des Jüngeren (Les Dessins de Hans Holbein le Jeune).* Published by Paul Ganz [1911-1926]. (II) *Die Handzeichnungen Hans Holbeins d.J.:Kritischer Katalog.* 1937.

[HOLMES]. *Portraits of Illustrious Personages of the Court of Henry VIII. Reproduced in Imitation of the Original Drawings of Hans Holbein in the Collection of Her Majesty.* I and II Series. With notes by R. R. Holmes (Hanfstaengl, s.a.).

[VERTUE]. *A Catalogue of the Collection of Pictures, &c., belonging to King James the Second: To which is added, A Catalogue of the Pictures and Drawings in the Closet of the late Queen Caroline, with their exact Measures; and also of the Principal Pictures in the Palace at Kensington, London, 1758.*

[WOLTMANN]. *Holbein und seine Zeit.* By Alfred Woltmann. Second edition, 1874. 2 Vols.

[WORNUM]. *Some Account of the Life and Works of Hans Holbein, Painter, of Augsburg.* By Ralph Nicholson Wornum. 1867.

Catalogue	Windsor	Vertue	Chamberlaine, ed. 1812	Wornum	Woltmann	Arundel	Holmes	Braun	Ganz I	Ganz II
Frontispiece	12188	37	—	—	272	—	—	—	XI, 7	129
1	12224	182	(47)	p. 402, 6	275	I, 2	I, 4	23	XIV, 4	26
2	12225	125	—	p. 402, 4	274	I, 3	II, 18	—	XXIV, 9	18
3	12268	6	(48)	p. 401, 3	273	V, 1	I, 3	24	XXXVI, 2	25
4	12228	25	(14)	p. 412, 34	278	—	I, 5	—	I, 4	28
5	12269	96	(1)	p. 409, 12	279	I, 5	I, 6	27	XXXIII, 9	31
6	12226	150	(49)	p. 407, 42	276	I, 4	I, 7	25	XII, 4	27
7	12270	27	(8)	p. 412, 35	277	IV, 15	I, 8	26	XIX, 3	30
8	12229	98	(41)	p. 413, 40	280	IV, 11	I, 9	28	II, 4	29
9	12217	181	(6)	p. 409, 14	353	V, 15	I, 10	—	XIV, 5	34
10	12266	3	(35)	p. 401, 1	282	II, 14	I, 11	16	XIII, 7	20
11	12273	9	(3)	p. 409, 13	355	V, 16	II, 11	—	XVII, 4	32
12	12272	73	(79)	p. 401, 2	281	I, 1	I, 12	49	XVIII, 3	19
13	12205	151	(62)	p. 404, 24	283	IV, 1	I, 13	12	XII, 7	35
14	12204	183	(31)	p. 410, 19	285	III, 8	I, 39	11	XV, 3	59
15	12203	157	(30)	p. 406, 34	284	III, 7	I, 38	10	XXV, 5	60
16	12212	136	(61)	p. 409, 17	324	—	II, 23	—	XXV, 9	77
17	12215	171	(75)	p. 408, 6	314	II, 4	I, 20	—	I, 5	84
18	12214	202	(76)	p. 410, 24	330	II, 3	I, 22	46	XXXI, 10	83
19	12236	8	(57)	p. 409, 15	337	III, 6	I, 29	32	XIX, 4	74
20	12219	11	(42)	p. 411, 26	336	II, 9	I, 28	20	VIII, 10	66
21	12222	22	(45)	p. 410, 20	339	IV, 8	II, 16	22	XXI, 5	68
22	12265	35	(34)	p. 405, 31	286	I, 9	I, 36	15	X, 5	62
23	12263	33	(50)	p. 404, 21	288	II, 11	I, 16	29	IX, 10	70
24	12245	17	(77)	p. 405, 26	320	IV, 6	I, 23	47	XXVI, 8	85
25	12247	10	(78)	p. 411, 30	321	I, 13	I, 24	48	XXXVI, 9	86
26	12227	4	(36)	0. 411, 25	333	III, 12	II, 12	17	XXX, 9	63
27	12257	186	(12)	p. 413, 38	350	V, 10	II, 24	—	XXXV, 9	94
28	12209	132	(26)	p. 409, 16	332	II, 11	II, 14	7	—	—
29	12216	13	—	p. 406, 35	313	V, 2	I, 21	45	—	—
30	12246	137	—	p. 407, 41	322	I, 12	I, 31	—	XXXIX, 5	C4
31	12237	21	(58)	p. 403, 17	308	II, 13	I, 48	33	XXIX, 8	75
32	12258	155	(71)	p. 403, 12	345	V, 4	I, 52	—	XIV, 6	91
33	12259	130	(9)	p. 406, 33	348	V, 6	I, 50	—	XXXIII, 10	41

Catalogue	Windsor	Vertue	Chamberlaine, ed. 1812	Wornum	Woltmann	Arundel	Holmes	Braun	Ganz I	Ganz II
34	12234	83	(55)	p. 404, 19	300	I, 6	I, 37	—	XXVII, 10	40
35	12208	172	(33)	p. 403, 15	309	IV, 9	I, 49	14	VI, 2	61
36	12249	167	(81)	p. 403, 13	307	III, 16	I, 35	—	—	—
37	12192	200	(16)	p. 405, 30	311	II, 15	I, 54	4	XXI, 4	42
38	12242	31	(70)	p. 404, 20	304	I, 10	I, 34	42	XVI, 2	45
39	12267	72	(65)	p. 410, 22	325	III, 1	I, 1	38	XXV, 8	44
40	12193	187	(17)	p. 410, 23	341	—	II, 21	3	XIX, 5	54
41	12220	126	(43)	p. 413, 39	331	III, 4	II, 15	21	—	—
42	12198	129	(22)	p. 406, 38	305	IV, 3	II, 5	6	X, 8	56
43	12244	86	(67)	p. 406, 32	294	II, 8	II, 6	43	XXVIII, 9	43
44	12260	160	(2)	p. 405, 25	346	V, 3	I, 51	—	XV, 5	92
45	12255	153	(11)	p. 412, 33	352	V, 8	I, 43	—	XV, 4	95
46	12200	14	(27)	p. 407, 1	326	—	—	—	XXVII, 8	47
47	12190	—	(21)	p. 413, —	357	V, 13	II, 2	—	XVI, 4	96
48	12256	18	(10)	p. 408, 11	356	V, 14	I, 44	—	XXIX, 9	97
49	12254	12	(5)	p. 411, 29	354	V, 11	I, 45	—	XXX, 8	98
50	12210	152	(37)	p. 408, 7	302	III, 9	I, 40	18	XVI, 3	64
51	12211	185	(38)	p. 408, 10	335	III, 10	I, 41	19	—	—
52	12243	169	(25)	p. 403, 16	310	III, 11	I, 18	—	XIX, 6	81
53	12195	184	(23)	p. 407, 44	315	II, 12	I, 19	—	X, 7	57
54	12233	199	(56)	p. 402, 9	301	I, 8	I, 47	31	XVII, 5	73
55	12271	91	(60)	p. 412, 37	319	II, 6	II, 10	35	XXVII, 9	76
56	12194	1	(74)	p. 410, 21	334	I, 15	I, 26	44	I, 3	82
57	12231	74	(51)	p. 408, 5	316	IV, 2	I, 15	30	XII, 8	72
58	12191	5	(13)	p. 411, 31	342	IV, 4	II, 27	1	VIII, 9	52
59	12199	84	(24)	p. 406, 37	287	III, 13	I, 53	—	X, 6	58
60	12223	170	(46)	p. 412, 32	340	IV, 6	II, 22	—	XXV, 10	69
61	12253	156	—	p. 413, 41	351	V, 9	—	—	XXXVI, 7	99
62	12218	2	(39)	p. 408, 9	329	IV, 12	I, 42	—	XXIX, 10	65
63	12189	154	(15)	p. 410, 18	323	II, 1	I, 25	2	XVII, 6	53
64	12250	85	(82)	p. 403, 18	289	IV, 10	I, 32a	50	XVIII, 4	88
65	12251	198	—	p. 407, 40	290	—	I, 32b	—	XX, 7	C5
66	12206	29	(69)	p. 402, 5	291	I, 16	I, 17	41	—	—
67	12264	93	(18)	p. 412, 37	343	II, 10	II, 13	5	XVIII, 5	50
68	12221	131	(44)	p. 403, 14	317	IV, 7	II, 7	—	XXIII, 4	67
69	12239	128	(63)	p. 402, 7	296	IV, 5	I, 14	36	XXXV, 10	78
70	12240	161	(64)	p. 407, 4	297	III, 5	—	37	XXVI, 10	79
71	12201	20	(28)	p. 407, 2	327	III, 2	I, 2	8	XXII, 4	49
72	12252	15	(68)	p. 411, 27	344	II, 16	I, 30	40	XXVIII, 10	89
73	12230	19	(52)	p. 411, 28	338	II, 7	I, 27	—	XXIV, 10	71
74	12262	168	(7)	p. 406, 39	349	V, 5	II, 17	—	—	—
75	12241	16	(66)	p. 404, 23	306	IV, 12	II, 4	39	XXX, 10	80
76	12197	201	(19)	p. 402, 11	292	III, 15	II, 8	—	XX, 8	C2
77	12196	138	(20)	p. 405, 28	293	III, 14	II, 20	—	XXXVI, 5	55
78	12207	23	(32)	p. 404, 22	298	IV, 14	I, 33	13	—	—
79	12248	133	(80)	p. 402, 10	295	II, 14	II, 3	—	—	—
80	12238	127	(59)	p. 402, 8	318	II, 5	II, 9	34	—	—
81	12232	188	(53)	p. 405, 27	303	IV, 13	I, 46	—	—	—
82	12261	75	(4)	p. 405, 29	347	V, 7	II, 25	—	—	—
83	12213	134	(40)	p. 408, 8	312	II, 2	II, 19	—	—	—
84	12235	135	(54)	p. 406, 36	299	I, 7	II, 25	—	—	—
85	12202	7	(29)	p. 407, 3	328	III, 3	II, 1	9	—	—

INDEX OF NAMES

PLATES

I. SIR JOHN MORE

2. SIR THOMAS MORE

Tho: Moor L'Chancelour.

3. SIR THOMAS MORE

The Lady Barkley.

4. ELIZABETH DAUNCEY

5. CECILY HERON

6. JOHN MORE THE YOUNGER

7. ANNE CRESACRE

Mother Iak.

8. MARGARET GIGGS

9. A WOMAN: UNKNOWN

Harry Guldeford Knight.

10. SIR HENRY GUILDFORD

11. A WOMAN: UNKNOWN

12. WILLIAM WARHAM, ARCHBISHOP OF CANTERBURY

13. CARDINAL FISHER, BISHOP OF ROCHESTER

The Lady Eliot.

14. MARGARET, LADY ELYOT

15. SIR THOMAS ELYOT

16. MARY, DUCHESS OF RICHMOND AND SOMERSET

17. HENRY HOWARD, EARL OF SURREY

18. FRANCES, COUNTESS OF SURREY

19. LADY RATCLIFFE

The Lady Lister.

20. JANE, LADY LISTER

The Lady Meutas.

21. JOAN, LADY MEUTAS

22. SIR JOHN GODSALVE

23. THOMAS BOLEYN, EARL OF WILTSHIRE (?)

24. THOMAS, LORD VAUX

The Lady Vaux.

25. ELIZABETH, LADY VAUX

26. MARY, LADY HEVENINGHAM (?)

27. A LADY: UNKNOWN

28. MARGARET, MARCHIONESS OF DORSET

29. HENRY HOWARD, EARL OF SURREY

30. THOMAS, LORD VAUX

Reskemeer a Cornish Gent:

31. WILLIAM RESKIMER

32. A GENTLEMAN: UNKNOWN

33. A GENTLEMAN: UNKNOWN

34. SIR NICHOLAS POYNTZ

35. SIMON GEORGE OF QUOCOUTE

36. SIR CHARLES WINGFIELD

Nicholas Borbonius Poeta.

37. NICHOLAS BOURBON THE ELDER

Rich Southwell Knight.

ANNO   ETTATIS SVA
                              · 3 3

38. SIR RICHARD SOUTHWELL

39. QUEEN JANE SEYMOUR

40. LADY BOROUGH (?)

41. A LADY (PRINCESS MARY ?)

42. EDWARD, LORD CLINTON

43. SIR THOMAS STRANGE

44. A GENTLEMAN: UNKNOWN

45. A LADY: UNKNOWN

46. EDWARD, PRINCE OF WALES

47. A LADY: UNKNOWN

48. A LADY: UNKNOWN

49. A LADY: UNKNOWN

Phillip Hobbie Knight

50. SIR PHILIP HOBY

The Lady Hobbei.

51. LADY HOBY (?)

52. EDWARD STANLEY, EARL OF DERBY

53. GEORGE BROOKE, LORD COBHAM

54. JOHN POYNTZ

The Lady Rich.

55. ELIZABETH, LADY RICH

56. KATHARINE, DUCHESS OF SUFFOLK

57. WILLIAM PARR, MARQUESS OF NORTHAMPTON

58. ELIZABETH, LADY AUDLEY (?)

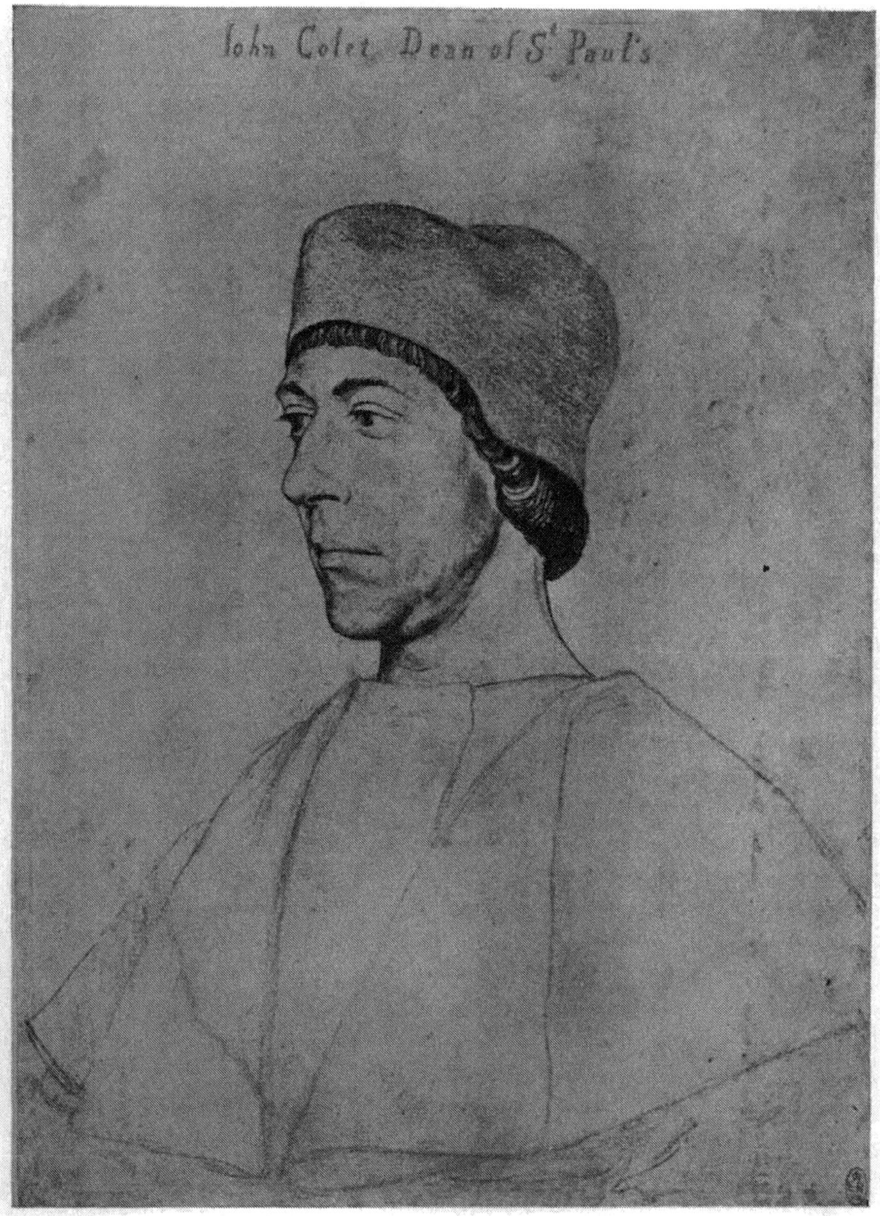
Iohn Colet Dean of St Paul's

59. AN ECCLESIASTIC: UNKNOWN

The Lady Montegle.

60. MARY, LADY MONTEAGLE

61. A LADY: UNKNOWN

62. A LADY : UNKNOWN

Anna Bollein Queen.

63. A LADY: UNKNOWN

64. SIR THOMAS WYATT

65. SIR THOMAS WYATT (*Copy*)

66. WILLIAM FITZWILLIAM, EARL OF SOUTHAMPTON

The Lady Buts.

67. MARGARET, LADY BUTTS

Phil: Melanchton.

68. A MAN : UNKNOWN

I Russell L Privy Seale.   with one Eye

69. JOHN RUSSELL, EARL OF BEDFORD

70. LORD FRANCIS RUSSELL

71. EDWARD, PRINCE OF WALES (?)

72. MARY ZOUCH (?)

The Lady Parker.

73. GRACE, LADY PARKER (?)

74. A GENTLEMAN: UNKNOWN

75. SIR WILLIAM SHARINGTON

76. SIR GEORGE CAREW

77. SIR GAVIN CAREW

78. SIR JOHN GAGE

Lᵈ Wentworth.

79. THOMAS, BARON WENTWORTH

80. RICHARD, BARON RICH

81. SIR THOMAS PARRY

82. A GENTLEMAN: UNKNOWN (*Not by Holbein*)

83. HENRY HOWARD, EARL OF SURREY (*Not by Holbein*)

84. A GENTLEMAN: UNKNOWN (*Not by Holbein*)

85. EDWARD, PRINCE OF WALES (*Not by Holbein*)

CONTENTS

CPSIA information can be obtained
at www.ICGtesting.com
Printed in the USA
BVHW052023191221
624302BV00004B/50